INDIAN MOUNDS OF THE MIDDLE OHIO VALLEY

INDIAN MOUNDS
OF THE MIDDLE OHIO VALLEY:

A Guide to
Adena and Ohio Hopewell Sites

Susan L. Woodward
and
Jerry N. McDonald

The McDonald & Woodward Publishing Company
Blacksburg, Virginia
1986

M⊕W

The McDonald & Woodward Publishing Company
Guides to the American Landscape

INDIAN MOUNDS OF THE MIDDLE OHIO VALLEY:
A Guide to Adena and Ohio Hopewell Sites

95 94 93 92 91 90   10 9 8 7 6 5 4 3 2
First printing, December 1986
Second printing, April 1989

Library of Congress Catalog Number: 86-62694
ISBN O-939923-00-9
Printed in the United States of America
by Book Crafters, Chelsea, Michigan

A WORD TO USERS OF THIS BOOK

This book is the first title to be issued in the "Guides to the American Landscape" series. We hope that this book and others in the series will provide a useful service in helping readers to become more familiar with specific regions, or natural and cultural themes, that are parts of the land and legacy of North America. In particular, we hope to provide a general understanding of the nature of each region or theme, detailed information about how to visit and more thoroughly experience the places, and sources of additional information about each specific subject.

In order to assess how well our guidebooks are meeting these objectives we would appreciate hearing from readers who have used this book. What did you like — and what didn't you like — about it? What improvements would you recommend be incorporated into a revised version of this particular book? Have we overlooked sites that could have been included? Would you use another guidebook in this series if it related to a place or theme in which you were interested? Would you like a list of other titles published or scheduled for publication in the near future?

The McDonald & Woodward Publishing Company
P. O. Box 10308
Blacksburg, Virginia 24062-0308

Errata

page 28: lines 11 and 12 – "notably...Albert Gallatin" should read "notably from such men as Samuel G. Morton and Samuel F. Haven."

page 35: first paragraph, line 1 – "Ad" should read "Adena."

page 64: first paragraph, line 5 – "Massie" should read "Massies."

third paragraph, line 5 – "NW" should read "NE."

throughout: "Ephriam Squier" should read "Ephraim Squier."

Ohio Historical Society telephone number has been changed and should read "614-297-2300."

ACKNOWLEDGMENTS

Many people and organizations within the Illinois-Kentucky-Massachusetts triangle assisted in our compilation of information for use in this book, and we sincerely thank each of them for their contribution. All have helped to make this a better publication. In particular, however, we would like to acknowledge the assistance of the following people who were extraordinarily helpful in providing us with detailed information about multiple sites and directing us to, or through, archival materials: Kenneth Apschnikat (Mound City Group National Monument), Jim Bloemker (West Virginia Department of Culture and History), John Dietz (Columbus Department of Recreation and Parks), Robert Maslowski (U. S. Army Corps of Engineers, Huntington, West Virginia), Ron Mills (Ohio Division of Parks), Arlene Peterson (Ohio Historical Society), Franco Ruffini (Ohio Office of Historic Preservation), Thomas Sanders (Kentucky Heritage Council), and Al Tonetti (Ohio Office of Historic Preservation). We also thank Kenneth Apschnikat and Jerry Chilton of Mound City Group National Monument and Martha Potter Otto of the Ohio Historical Society for reading and providing critical comments about an earlier version of parts of this book.

CONTENTS

MOUNDS AS LANDSCAPE FEATURES

There seemed to come to me a picture as of a distant time, and with it came a demand for an interpretation of this mystery. The unknown must become known.

Frederic Ward Putnam, 1888,
upon viewing Serpent Mound

Mounds and earthworks constitute the most conspicuous record of prehistoric American Indian culture to be found on the landscape of eastern North America. As such, these earthen and stone artifacts can provide both silent testimony of and appreciable insight into ways of life that are at once gone but inescapably parts of the cultural legacy of eastern North America. At one time tens, perhaps hundreds, of thousands of these artifacts, present in diverse forms, sizes, levels of complexity and concentrations, occurred between the Atlantic seaboard and the Great Plains, and between southeastern Canada and the Gulf of Mexico. Most of the mounds and earthworks that were present two centuries ago, however, have been destroyed as a result of the tranformation of eastern North America into agricultural, urban and transportation landscapes. Fortunately, a small number of mounds and earthworks have survived to the present, and thus provide the modern observer with the opportunity to experience, first hand, physical expressions of cultural values and lifeways now vanished.

Study of the mounds and earthworks over the last two hundred years has shown that — despite a century of some widespread and well-entrenched opinions to the contrary — these artifacts were built by American Indians, not by a Lost Race of civilized Mound Builders. In fact, not one widespread, homogeneous group, but several different groups of Indians built the mounds and earthworks at different times and for different reasons. One of the earliest of the mound building groups were the Adena Indians who appeared in the middle Ohio Valley around 2,500-3,000 years ago and probably occupied that area for 750-1,000 years. About 2,000-2,500 years ago another group of mound builders — the Ohio Hopewell — appeared in part of the Adena homeland and persisted there for 500-750 years. Then, around 1,000 years ago, Indians possessing Mississippian cultural characteristics appeared in the middle Ohio Valley and remained for 600-700 years. The Adena and Hopewell Indians built distinctive, and sometimes very impressive, burial mounds, effigy mounds, geometric earthworks, and fort-like structures. Indians of the Mississippian cultures built pyramidal or truncated-pyramidal temple mounds in the southeastern

1

United States and along the Mississippi River, and might have done the same in the middle Ohio Valley. The precision, grace, frequency and magnitude of effort represented by these mounds and earthworks requires that they be ranked among the important prehistoric engineering — and artistic — accomplishments of mankind.

This book is a guide to the extant mounds and earthworks built by the Adena and Ohio Hopewell Indians. Section I of this book provides an overview of Adena and Hopewell chronology, geography, ecology and culture, and reviews the ways in which mounds and earthworks have been perceived, studied, and managed by Americans during the last two centuries. Section II identifies and describes the extant, publicly accessible mounds, earthworks, and affiliated sites that preserve elements of the material culture and works of the Adena and Ohio Hopewell. Section III identifies sources of additional information about these two groups of Indians and the sites described in Section II.

The primary purpose of this book is to facilitate access by the interested public to information about the Adena and Hopewell Indians, and especially to help people become aware of, visit, experience, and learn more about mounds, earthworks, and affiliated sites. We see this as a versatile book, being of use to different groups of people with differing, but focused, interests in the archeological heritage of eastern North America — travelers, educators, students, archeologists, naturalists, recreation leaders, librarians, planners and anybody else with a curious mind and an interest in understanding and preserving the remaining record of North American prehistory.

SECTION I

MOUNDS IN ARCHEOLOGICAL AND
HISTORICAL CONTEXT

THE ADENA AND OHIO HOPEWELL INDIANS

The mound builders did not leave written records in books of their origins, achievements and beliefs, as do people of true civilizations. They left their records written on the land and in their bones and artifacts. So their histories must be reconstructed from the bits and pieces which have survived the ravages of weather and time and of their successors on the land. Of these bits and pieces we have only a small sample — those earthworks, mounds, burials, and habitations which have been discovered and systematically investigated, described and analyzed. In the 200 years that English-speaking people have been aware of the mound builders' legacy, opinions as to their origins, intentions, and demise have appeared and changed as new information became available, new attitudes developed, and new theories appeared. There is still no concensus on how these cultures arose or why they vanished, but there is enough information that we can provide a general outline of the times and places of their existence, and some of the distinguishing characteristics of the different mound building cultures.

The Adena and the Classical, or Ohio, Hopewell are the two most prominent mound building cultures known from the middle Ohio Valley. Mounds built by Late Woodland and Mississippian groups are present in the region, but these are rare. Both the Adena and Hopewell cultures represent regional expressions of a mortuary (death and burial) cult widespread in eastern North America, the Adena being the simpler and earlier elaboration and the Hopewell representing the later, more elaborate expression of the cult. The names for these cultures were derived from two archeological sites in the Scioto River Valley near Chillicothe, Ohio — Adena from the Adena Estate of Ohio Governor Thomas Worthington and Hopewell from the farm of Captain M. C. Hopewell.

Chronological Position of the Adena and Hopewell in North American Prehistory

Four major culture stages, called Periods, are recognized for the prehistory of eastern North America (Figure 1). The earliest, the Paleo-Indian Period, encompasses the first people to inhabit the region — the specialized nomadic big-game hunters of about 12,000-8,000 years ago. With the extinction of the mammoths, mastodons, horses and other large mammals of the last Ice Age, human lifestyles changed and the second culture stage began, that of the Archaic. Archaic peoples were nomadic hunters, gatherers, and collectors that relied upon a great variety of plant and animal resources but who demonstrated an increasing tendency to establish more

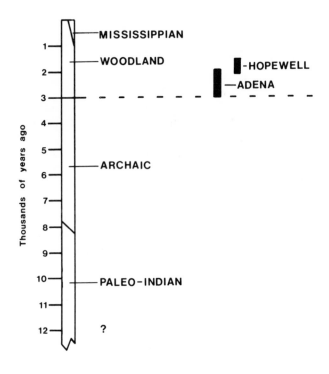

Figure 1. The place of the Adena and Ohio Hopewell Indians within the general chronology of North American Indians.

frequently used or long lasting habitations. It is among the people of the Archaic Period that the traits first appeared which came to characterize the Adena and Hopewell. Three major innovations took place late in the Archaic Period: the making of pottery, horticulture, and the burial of dead in earthen mounds. These practices, when fully developed, came to mark the third culture stage, the Woodland Period, which began about 3,000 years ago. The Woodland Period is divided into three divisions — Early, Middle and Late. The Adena are associated with the Early Woodland Period; the Hopewell with the Middle Woodland Period. The Woodland Period lasted until European contact was established in the 17th-18th centuries. In the southern and central Mississippi Valley and the southeastern United States another stage, the Mississippian Period, appeared about 1,200 years ago and survived over much of that region until European contact was established in the 16th-18th centuries. The Mississippian cultures are characterized by their construction of temple mounds, the development of permanent population clusters around ceremonial centers, and the presence and trappings of the Southern Death Cult.

6

The Adena and Hopewell Homeland

The territory occupied by the Adena Indians extended from southeastern Indiana to southwestern Pennsylvania, and from north central Ohio to central Kentucky (Figure 2). The Hopewell homeland was less extensive, being confined largely to the southwestern quarter of Ohio. The area occupied by the Adena included parts of three physiographic (landform) provinces: the Appalachian Plateau, the Interior Low Plateaus, and the Central Lowlands (Figure 3). The Hopewell were located primarily within, or very near, the Central Lowlands province, mostly along its southern and southeastern borders where it came into contact with the other two provinces. These provinces differed in several ways — including the nature of the land surface itself, the size and gradient of streams, soil quality, and the kinds of plants and animals to be found. Each of the provinces constituted an environment somewhat different from the others, with which the Adena or Hopewell interacted. These environments influenced many activities and decisions in Adena and Hopewell life, including — for example — the

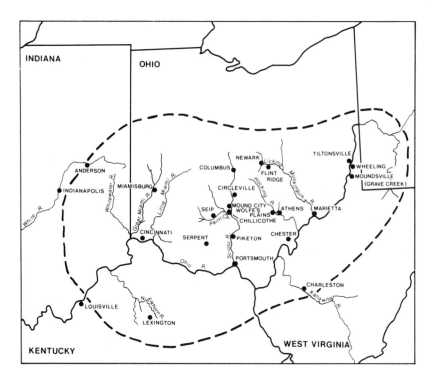

Figure 2. The Adena and Hopewell homelands, with place names mentioned in Section I.

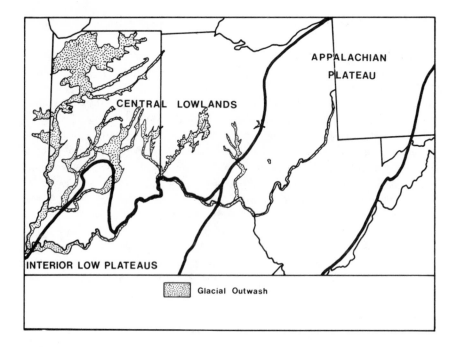

Figure 3. Physiography of the Adena and Ohio Hopewell homeland. Notice especially the extensive deposits of alluvium along tributaries of the Ohio River in the Central Lowlands Province.

size of population units and habitations, the quantity and variety of natural resources available, mobility, and the location at which different activities took place. The landform differences also influenced the type, number and location of mounds and earthworks that the Adena and Hopewell built. Yet, despite the differences among the provinces, the middle Ohio River and its tributaries appears to have been a major influence in unifying the Adena and Hopewell culture regions. The Hopewell appear to have occupied less diverse environments than the Adena, being restricted largely to wide alluvial valleys and bordering isolated uplands within the northwestern part of the middle Ohio Valley.

The heavily dissected Appalachian Plateau is characterized by numerous small hilltops and narrow ridges. Erosion resistant rocks, especially sandstones, have produced steep-sided valleys that occasionally contain rock shelters. Most floodplains along streams are narrow, if present at all. Consequently, large expanses of level land are relatively scarce in this province, especially in the eastern part. The sandstone-capped western edge of the Appalachian Plateau, especially from the vicinity of Circleville, Ohio, to northern Kentucky, is scarp-like and, in many places, is dissected to the extent that steep sided promontories and isolated buttes have formed.

8

The Interior Low Plateaus, consisting primarily of limestones in northern and central Kentucky and a small part of south central Ohio, present a surface that is more gently rounded than that of the Appalachian Plateau but more rolling than that of the Central Lowlands. Wide flood plains, however, are also uncommon along streams in this region.

The Central Lowlands in southern Ohio and Indiana are relatively level, having been covered with glacial ice and coated with till debris on one or more occasions during the Quaternary Period (the last 1.8 million years) — most recently between about 20,000 and 12,000 years ago. The spread of glaciers across this and adjacent areas also caused changes in the regional drainage patterns. In particular, the Ohio River drainage was enlarged considerably. Prior to glaciation, the Ohio River headwaters were in the vicinity of Louisville, Kentucky. After glaciation, the Ohio River headwaters arose along a line extending from southern New York to northwestern North Carolina. In addition to changing the direction of flow, glaciation also changed the character of the Ohio River's north bank tributaries in other ways. Meltwater carried vast quantities of sediment from the glacier front and deposited substantial volumes of this material in the river valleys, thus creating wide flood plains (Figure 3). Subsequent downcutting by the streams created a system of terraces in the valleys — tiers of level land at different elevations above stream level (Figure 4).

The Adena and Hopewell people existed in climatic and biotic conditions generally similar to those that exist in the middle Ohio Valley today. The average annual temperatures might have been warmer than those of today but, if so, only slightly. The vegetation of the region was dominated by the Central Hardwood Forest, a forest that contained diverse species of trees, shrubs, vines and non-woody plants, including such economically

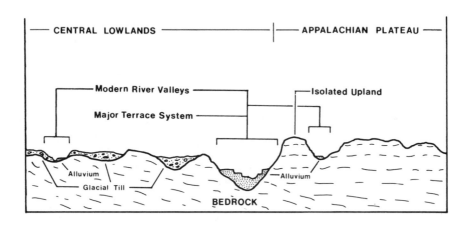

Figure 4. A generalized cross section through the Central Lowlands-Appalachian Plateau border region in southern Ohio.

important species as blackberries, walnuts, oaks, paw-paws, and hickories. A great variety of economically important species of animals — such as whitetail deer, elk, black bear, wild turkey, box turtles, cottontail rabbits, etc. — was associated with this forest. The favorable climate and great plant and animal diversity provided a productive environment in which the Adena and Hopewell Indians could function with relative security as hunters, gatherers, and collectors. If the Adena and Hopewell practiced horticulture — and tenuous evidence suggests that they did, although perhaps on a small scale — the best environmental conditions for this activity probably would have occurred in the Central Lowlands where there was the best combination of level land, alluvial soils, and long growing season.

In some parts of the Adena and Hopewell homeland, such as where different physiographic provinces meet or alluvial valleys interface with uplands, the different local environments likely would have resulted in a relatively greater variety of plant and animal resources than would occur in less diverse regions. These areas also would have provided a relatively greater variety of other natural resources than would be available in less diverse regions. The regions with greater local diversity, perhaps, would have been more likely to be productive over extended periods of time, to have supported relatively larger populations of Indians than would less diverse locations, and to have permitted the accumulation of wealth and the development of more well defined social classes among some Indian societies. Such conditions might have existed along the Scioto, Licking, and Great Miami rivers — where the best conditions for horticulture, travel, and trade probably also occurred — and could have given rise to larger populations, the accumulation of greater wealth, the development of more centralized class-oriented social and religious organization, and the creation of more elaborate mound and earthwork complexes.

The correspondence between the landforms of these three provinces and the types and locations of mounds and earthworks is significant. Adena burial mounds are found over the largest area and in the greatest variety of sites. Normally, these burial mounds were placed on hilltops, ridgetops, benches or higher terraces overlooking major tributaries of the Ohio River. Occasionally, however, Adena burial mounds were built on lower terraces, especially in the Appalachian Plateau where wide flood plains occasionally existed (as at Charleston and Moundsville, West Virginia). These floodplains provided relatively large areas of level land and great quantities of the clay, sand, and gravel used in the construction of the mounds. Adena earthworks (circles), however, were usually built on more extensive level land and thus were less common in the Appalachian Plateau (although important works were located at Charleston, West Virginia and Wolfe's Plains, Ohio) than the Interior Low Plateaus or Central Lowlands (with important centers near Anderson, Indiana; Lexington, Kentucky; and Chillicothe, Ohio). Hopewell geometric earthworks and burial mounds are almost always located on the second or third terraces of major river valleys

— most notably those of the Scioto River (and its tributary Paint Creek) and the Great Miami River. Here again, the extensive terraces provided relatively large expanses of flat land and an abundance of easily accessible sediments for use in mound and earthwork construction. Hopewell fort-like enclosures, however, were typically located atop isolated erosional remnants (e.g., Fort Hill) or nearly isolated promontories (e.g., Fort Ancient).

The Adena Indians (circa 1,000 B.C. to A.D. 100)

Major concentrations of Adena Indians appear to have been located in the central Scioto Valley near Chillicothe, Ohio; the Kanawha Valley near Charleston, West Virginia; the central Hocking Valley near Athens, Ohio; and the upper Ohio Valley south of Wheeling, West Virginia. Peripheral clusters occurred in the Great Miami River drainage in southwestern Ohio; along the North Elkhorn River near Lexington, Kentucky; and along the White River near Anderson, Indiana.

The Adena apparently lived in very small, widely scattered hamlets which are not well represented in the archeological record. There is good evidence that they also occupied rock shelters and caves, features that were relatively numerous in the Appalachian Plateau and Interior Low Plateaus, at least on a temporary basis — perhaps in the winter or during periods of inclement weather. Many Early Adena mounds were located on hilltops near overhanging ledges which provided habitation sites.

Adena were hunters and gatherers primarily, although they seem to have practiced some horticulture. Known to them were some of the earliest domesticated plants known in North America: goosefoot (*Chenopodium*), sumpweed (*Iva*), canary grass (*Phalaris*), and sunflower (*Helianthus*). They also had acquired two crop species from Mexico: gourd (*Lagenaria*) and squash (*Cucurbita*). Maize (*Zea mays*) was introduced only in Late Adena time; the earliest radiocarbon date on maize from an Adena site is 280 ± 140 years B.C. (from Daines Mound II in the Hocking Valley, Athens County, Ohio). The common bean (*Phaseolus*), which with maize and squash formed the traditional triumvirate of Native American horticulture, was unknown during the Adena (and Hopewell) period.

The Adena Culture represented a major departure from Archaic cultures in that Adena people buried their dead in *artificial* earthen mounds. Adena has its antecedents among its Late Archaic neighbors to the north and west, the Red Ochre Culture and the Glacial Kame Culture, who placed burials in *natural* ridges and hills. The Adena retained some burial practices of the contemporary Red Ochre Culture, including the use of red ochre paint on burials, the placing of artifacts with burials, and the practice of cremation. Even "Adena" stemmed and "Adena" leaf-shaped blades were used by Red Ochre people. Adena mound building was an innovation, but it was superimposed on an existing burial complex. It made a difference — or

11

perhaps reflected a difference — in lifestyle. The use of burial mounds tended to concentrate the dead in one location. Adena mounds were used over and over, possibly for generations, and represent a commitment to a particular place as well as a form of subsistence which allowed for at least semipermanent settlement.

Adena burial mounds are typically conical (Figure 5) and contain multiple burials. The dead were prepared for burial in various ways. Sometimes the bones were defleshed before burial by exposing the corpses to carrion feeders on scaffolds, trees, or temporary graves. The cleaned bones were then collected and either placed directly in permanent burials or cremated, then buried. Still other burials consisted of laying the corpse on its back in a nonflexed (i.e., fully extended) position. Early Adena graves were lined with bark. In Late Adena mounds log tombs are found. Initial burials were made in shallow pits in the original ground surface, then covered with earth. Each successive burial within a given mound was covered with more earth, and the mound grew in size over the years (Figure 6). The largest, represented today by the Miamisburg Mound (Ohio) and the Grave Creek Mound (West Virginia), were almost 70′ high.

Figure 5. The Adena Mound, a typical Early Woodland conical burial mound and the namesake of the Adena culture, prior to the salvage excavation of the site in 1901. This mound was located on Adena, originally the estate of Ohio politician Thomas Worthington, immediately west of Chillicothe, Ohio. The mound was removed because it was an impediment to agriculture (Ohio Historical Society photograph).

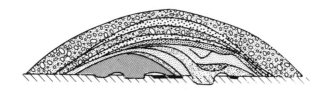

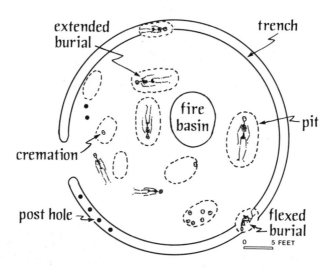

Figure 6. Representative views of Adena mound structure, based upon the Cresap Mound, Marshall County, West Virginia. (Top): Cross-section through mound illustrating that the mound was built up in increments. (Bottom): Floor plan, showing multiple extended and cremated burials prior to construction of the initial mound (after Dragoo, 1963).

Adena mounds were sometimes built over earlier occupation sites, so that in the floors of the mounds were preserved the postmolds of Adena dwellings (Figure 7). Story Mound in Chillicothe, Ohio, provided archeologists with the first documentation of the circular floor plan characteristic of Adena houses. Early Adena houses were constructed of evenly spaced single posts, and the walls leaned outward. They might have had a conical roof. Late Adena houses, still circular, were of double post construction; that is, the wall posts were set in pairs.

The burial cult of the Adena evolved through time and became more elaborate. It is possible to distinguish between Early Adena and Late Adena on the basis of artifacts and earthwork structures as well as the tomb and house construction mentioned above. Adena grave goods tended to be either tools or personal adornments and, especially when compared with

Figure 7. Adena house with side cut away to show postulated floor plan (after Dragoo, 1963).

Figure 8. Engraved Adena tablets.

the Hopewell, are relatively few in number. Items distinctive to the Adena include projectile points, tubular pipes, stone gorgets, and stone tablets (Table 1).

Tubular pipes were made of fireclay (pipestone). This occurred in large deposits in southern Ohio, especially east of the Scioto River. Early Adena pipes were cigar-shaped or plain tubes, often with one end blocked. A few Late Adena pipes were carved in effigies, the most famous individual specimen being the unique effigy of a human dwarf found in the Adena Mound itself.

Copper ornaments were made of rolled native copper probably obtained through trade from the Great Lakes region. We know that the Adena were involved in an extensive trade network, at least indirectly, because Adena pipes of Ohio pipestone and Adena points of Flint Ridge flint are found in sites well beyond the geographic range of the Adena themselves. Adena artifacts have turned up in the Chesapeake Bay area, Vermont, and New Brunswick.

Gorgets were ornaments worn around the neck. Early types were rectangular with 2 holes drilled at the center through which a cord could pass. These highly polished stones were concave on all four sides. In later gorgets the concavities were exaggerated making the gorget reel-shaped. What have been identified as expanded-center bar "gorgets" found in Late Adena burials, however, might have been atlatl weights and not ornaments at all.

Finally there are the unique stone tablets. These were small sandstone or siltstone slabs which apparently were used as whetstones to sharpen bone awls and to reduce chunks of hematite to red ochre paint. With use, deep grooves formed on the tablets. Early Adena tablets had rough, irregular edges. However, the red ochre was important in the burial ritual; and the tablets themselves seem to have assumed ceremonial significance. Late Adena tablets were carefully shaped, usually into rectangles (formal type). The highest refinement in tablet design came with the development of engraved tablets. On one side of these tablets was a geometric or zoomorphic *bas relief* (effigy type) (Figure 8). The opposite side was still grooved and used to prepare the paint.

The evolution of the Adena burial complex is also reflected in the appearance of a new and distinctive form of earthwork during Late Adena time — the "sacred circle." The typical sacred circle was a circular enclosure 150'-200' in diameter. The embankment was broken by one gateway. A ditch was excavated along the inside of the embankment, except at the gateway, where the surface was left undisturbed to form a causeway to an interior platform. Often these circles were built in clusters of 2 to 8, such as was found in the Wolfe's Plains Group near Athens, Ohio, or the Mt. Horeb Earthworks (Adena Park) near Lexington, Kentucky. Some of the circles enclosed burial mounds; some did not. The function of the sacred circle is

Table 1: Some Typical Adena and Hopewell Burial Goods

	Early Adena	Late Adena	Hopewell
Projectile points	"Adena" leaf "Adena" stemmed	"Robbins" leaf "Robbins" stemmed	—
Tubular pipes	Plain	Effigy (rare)	—
Platform pipes	—	—	Plain and effigy
Ornaments	Rolled copper beads	C-shaped copper bracelets	Mica; shell and pearl beads; copper ear spools
Gorgets	Slate: quadriconcave	Slate: reel-shaped and expanded center bar	Copper
Stone tablets	Crude, irregular outlines	Formal and effigy	—

not known; they may have served as meeting or ritual places for certain social groups or clans, or they may have served other purposes.

The Hopewell Indians (circa 150 B.C. to A.D. 500)

The Hopewell culture in many ways appears to be an elaboration of the Late Adena culture marked by more abundant, finely crafted, exotic grave goods and a greater complexity in earthwork design. Yet there exist traits in Hopewell culture with no antecedents in Adena, such as the platform pipe and the square house type, which suggest that the Hopewell was an independent and perhaps external development. The two cultures overlap in time for several hundred years, but it is unclear if they occupied the same geographic areas during that time span. Relics of Adena and Hopewell cultures have fascinated American anthropology and archeology since these disciplines first developed, yet there is still no consensus on the relationship between the two. Did Adena influence Hopewell, or vice versa? Or was it mutual, or even independent, stimulation which led to the flowering of both?

Even defining Hopewell culture has been problematical, because some elements of its burial practices are extremely widespread in North America. Some archeologists view Hopewell as a religious cult rather than a culture, per se, and compare it to the World of Islam, which encompasses so many, often quite different locally developed cultures today. The Hopewell cult — if that is what it was — was integrated through a huge trading network which extended from the Rocky Mountains to the Atlantic Ocean, from the Great Lakes to the Gulf of Mexico. This region is designated by some archeologists as the "Hopewell interaction sphere".

Whatever the definition, it is agreed that Hopewell reached its greatest — its classical — expression in the middle Ohio Valley. Classical, or Ohio, Hopewell was imprinted on the land in great geometric earthworks at Newark and Portsmouth and in the smaller, but nonetheless impressive, complexes which dotted the bottomlands of the Great Miami River and Scioto River valleys in south central and southwestern Ohio (Figure 9). Buried in the land were the great artistic achievements of the Hopewell people and the mystery of their being.

Significant social and settlement pattern changes apparently accompanied the rise of Hopewell, although there seems to have been no major difference in subsistence patterns relative to the Adena, except perhaps a greater reliance on annuals and crops of the floodplains. Greater social organization is implied by the greater size and complexity of the Hopewell earthworks and in the burial rituals themselves. Hopewell burial mounds tend to contain fewer skeletons in finer tombs and with more luxurious grave goods than do Adena mounds. Three fourths of the Hopewell burials were cremations (Figure 10). Tomb burials in the flesh were presumedly

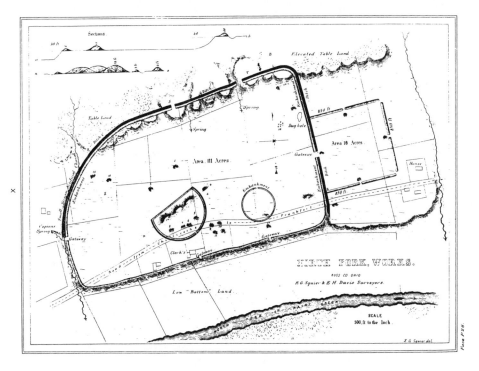

Figure 9. The Hopewell Group, namesake of the Hopewell culture, as depicted in Squier and Davis, 1848. This earthworks complex was located northwest of Chillicothe, Ohio, on the farm of Captain M. C. Hopewell, and is representative of the great number of Hopewell geometric earthworks that extended from Newark to Portsmouth and Cincinnati. Notice how the borders of this complex corresponded closely with the edges of the second terrace.

17

Figure 10. Hopewell crematory basin and obsidian grave offering, Mound No. 11, Hopewell Group. (Ohio Historical Society photograph.)

reserved for the highest social class (Figure 11). Much of the general population is not even represented in the mounds.

The Ohio Hopewell villages occupied lowland sites along major streams with broad bottomlands. The primary concentration was along the Scioto, but important centers also were developed in the Licking and Great Miami drainages. The earthworks complexes were situated on the second and third terraces of the rivers, well above normal flood danger yet still near the rivers which were so important for food, water, and transportation. The Hopewell did construct earthen and stone fort-like structures on isolated hilltops away from the rivers, but the classic Hopewell earthworks are associated with the bottomlands of the major waterways of southern Ohio.

Hopewell mound construction differed from that of the Adena. Hopewell mounds were often constructed as a single event, rather than in stages over a long period of time, and consequently were not as large as Adena mounds. The highest Hopewell mound (the central mound of the Hopewell Group, never reconstructed after excavation) was 33' high, and very few other mounds came near that height. Among surviving mounds, only Seip Mound (30' high) in Ross County approaches that height. The dead were prepared for burial in charnel houses. They seem often to have been dismembered and cremated in shallow crematory basins. The undestroyed bones were then collected and redeposited in individual graves in the charnel house floor, in anatomically correct order. A small amount of earth was

Figure 11. Hopewell extended burials from Mound 2, Hopewell Group. Both Adena and Hopewell used extended burials. Adena burials often included the use of bark (early) or log (late) tombs. Hopewell burials often included the use of stone tombs, as in one case above. Notice the presence of a large marine shell, obtained by long distance trade, near the skull of each skeleton. (Ohio Historical Society photograph.)

heaped over each grave. At some point, sometimes when space for additional burials was no longer available, the charnel house was dismantled and a mound was constructed over the crematory and associated graves. Hopewell buildings were typically square or rectangular, so the mounds covering the charnel house sites tended not to be conical like Adena mounds, but had ellipitical bases. Some, like the Tremper Mound in Scioto County, assumed very irregular shapes depending on the shape of the underlying structure (Figure 12).

Hopewell grave goods commonly consisted of materials imported from great distances and used only in fashioning funerary objects: fresh-water pearls, hammered copper and gold, galena, mica, conch shells, grizzly bear teeth, fossil shark teeth, obsidian (volcanic glass). Like the Adena, the Hopewell exchanged Flint Ridge flint and Ohio pipestone for these exotic materials. It is possible that different areas specialized in the production of different ceremonial and trade items. The Newark Earthworks complex, for example, may have been at the distribution center for flint from nearby Flint Ridge.

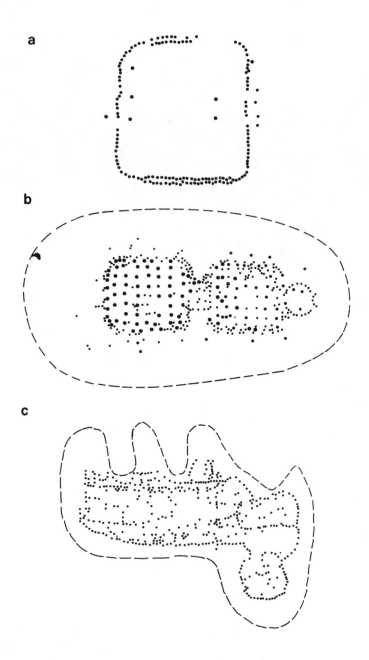

Figure 12. Floor plans of Hopewell workshops and charnel houses as revealed by post molds at Seip, Harness, and Tremper earthworks. (a): Hopewell workshops at Seip were round-cornered rectangles (after Baby and Langlois, 1979). (b): Hopewell charnel houses were normally slightly elongated rectangles, as at Harness Mound (after Greber, 1979). (c) The charnel house at Tremper was atypical in its irregular shape, but illustrates clearly how the shape of Hopewell mounds was influenced by the shape of the charnel houses (after Mills, 1916).

An emphasis on opulent, non-utilitarian grave goods and the fine craftsmanship and artistry of Hopewell ornaments distinguish Hopewell burials from Adena. Copper from Isle Royale in Lake Superior was hammered into breastplates and head dresses. Mica from the southern Appalachians was carved or cut into effigy forms (Figure 13) and sometimes used to blanket burials. Fresh-water pearls, perhaps from local streams or perhaps traded from the Wabash and Illinois rivers, were made into beads and strung in chains or sewn onto clothing. Pearls provide an excellent example of the wealth buried with some Hopewell individuals; over 100,000 were recovered from the Hopewell Group of mounds and 35,000 were found in a single cache at the Turner site in Hamilton County, Ohio. The 15,000 or so pearls covering a multiple burial in the large Seip Mound had an estimated value (if new and in good condition, as they were at the time of burial) equivalent to $2,000,000 in 1960.

Hopewell craftsmanship is well displayed in the many fine effigy platform pipes recovered from their mounds. Many forms of native wildlife — birds, amphibians, and mammals — are represented. One mound in the Mound City Group and the Tremper Mound yielded huge caches of these effigy pipes (Figure 14). The pipes were apparently produced by artisans

Figure 13. Hopewell craftsmen produced artistic cut-outs from thin sheets of mica. The mica was probably obtained from the middle Appalachian Mountains in North Carolina. These silhouettes — likenesses of a human hand, a projectile point, and the talon of a bird of prey — are from mounds in the Hopewell Group. (Ohio Historical Society photograph.)

Figure 14. A Hopewell effigy platform pipe from Mound 18, Mound City Group. (Ohio Historical Society photograph.)

that specialized in pipe making, and then entered into the trade network. Some pipes almost identical to each other have been discovered at widely separated localities.

The geometric enclosures — circles, squares, and octagons — are the most impressive and distinctive of the Hopewell earthworks. Some of these were quite large. The great circle at Newark, Ohio, is 1,200' in diameter and the octagon there encloses 50 acres. Some of the Hopewell earthworks complexes stretched for miles; the Newark earthworks covered about 4 square miles, while the earthworks at Portsmouth extended for about 8 miles in Ohio and Kentucky. Some researchers maintain that the Hopewell used a standard unit of measure (equivalent to about 57 meters) and knowledge of the right triangle to plan the configuration of their enclosures. Others are of the opinion that the earthworks served as lunar and solar observatories and that their alignments correspond with the declination of the moon or sun at various times of the year. Whether or not this is true, it seems that their functions were ceremonial. Sometimes the Hopewell villages were located outside the embankments near the earthworks, while at other times they were considerable distances from the earthworks.

The End Of Adena and Hopewell Mound Building

The disappearance of Hopewell (and, somewhat earlier, Adena), like its appearance, is not well understood. Various causes have been suggested, including cultural assimilation, prolonged drought, climatic cooling, epidemic disease, and warfare. The Adena might have been overwhelmed or absorbed by Hopewell culture. The hilltop enclosures, the "forts", of the Hopewell have been interpreted by some archeologists as last-stand defensive works. However, the disappearance of Hopewell around A.D. 500 precedes the appearance of fortified villages among other Middle Woodland groups in the middle Ohio Valley. Other archeologists regard the hilltop enclosures as ceremonial centers similar to the enclosures of the lowlands, and maintain that they could have been built over relatively long periods of time. Another suggested cause of the demise of the Hopewell is the collapse of the trade network due to social instability in non-Hopewell regions and the consequent loss of control over much of the continent's wealth by the Hopewell elite. Yet another opinion suggests that local populations could have become increasingly self-sufficient and thus had less reason to maintain long distance trade networks to obtain both essential resources and non-essential luxury goods.

MOUNDS DURING THE HISTORIC PERIOD

The earliest explorers, missionaries and settlers to enter the Ohio Valley from the English colonies along the Atlantic seaboard reported the existence of artificial earthworks in the forested land beyond the Appalachian Mountains. Some of these mounds were known to be burial features, while the function of others was unknown. Indians living in the Ohio Valley at the time that American settlement began had no knowledge of why, or when, the mounds had been built. As the number of American settlements increased in the Ohio Valley, more and more of the prehistoric earthworks became known, particularly because the new settlers selected many of the same sites upon which to build their villages that the Indians had earlier chosen as sites for their mounds and ceremonial centers. The clearing of the forest on these floodplains and terraces revealed the earthworks that, often, had been obscured by the forest. With continuing settlement and clearing, the number of mounds reported increased to levels that intrigued, perplexed and amazed informed people of the time. Curiosity about the mounds led to continued and expanded descriptions, visitations and explorations, and eventually to significant contributions to the development of archeology in North America.

Early American Perception of the Mounds

One of the earliest reactions of the American settlers to the mounds and earthworks they encountered was to name places after these features. Circleville, Ohio, was established within an earthworks complex containing two concentric circular embankments. Some of the streets of this community were laid out in circles, and were given names such as Circle Street and Circle Alley. Moundsville, West Virginia, derived its name from the Grave Creek Earthworks located there. The tendency to name after the mounds was widespread, was applied to many different elements of the cultural landscape, and continued through the years. Dozens of small towns and large cities in the middle Ohio Valley have a street named Mound or Moundview, whereas streets named Indian Mound, Mound Circle, Mound Terrace and others obviously derived from mounds also can be found. There are many Mound cemeteries, and among the parks in the middle Ohio Valley are Mound Park, Indian Mound(s) Park, Mounds State Park, Moundbuilders State Memorial, and Woodland Mound Park. Even businesses have adopted such names. The regal Miamisburg Mound overlooks the AEC's Mound Laboratory, while the telephone directory of Newark, Ohio, (nicknamed "Mound City") contains eleven businesses using Mound Builder(s) or Mound City as part of their name.

Even as early as the late part of the 18th Century, some mounds had become popular tourist attractions. Grave Creek Mound, near the Ohio River in what is today Moundsville, West Virginia, was perhaps the most famous of these early attractions. Nearly 70' high and located on a high terrace of the Ohio River floodplain, Grave Creek Mound dominated an important Adena and Hopewell mound and earthwork complex. As early as 1805, Meriwether Lewis reported finding the initials of numerous travelers carved in trees that were growing on and near the mound. Later, to enhance this mound's appeal to tourists, it was partly excavated and a museum was set up inside the excavation shaft. Even a bar was set up on top of the mound to slake the thirst of curious travelers. Grave Creek Mound later became the site of the Marshall County Fairgrounds, and is now the focal point of Grave Creek State Park.

One of the most enlightened reactions to the mounds and earthworks encountered by the new settlers took place at Marietta, Ohio. In 1788, leaders of the Ohio Company of Associates — just arrived from New England to settle in the Ohio Valley — formally acted to save part of the mound and earthworks complex they found at the site of their Marietta settlement. The two large enclosures and the great conical mound were set aside as public parks. Since that time, some parts of the park have given way to other needs, but, nonetheless, much of this unusual complex still remains — including the best example of a graded way (whose trace is preserved by the Sacra Via parkway), two truncated pyramid mounds, and the best surviving example of a moat-and-wall encircled conical burial mound.

Normally, however, mounds and earthworks were viewed passively and assigned relatively little importance. Occasionally, cemeteries were established around mounds — which were known to be burial features — and the mounds were thereby protected because the primary land use presented no physical theat to them. Mounds at Piketon, Tiltonsville, and Chester, Ohio, are examples of mounds that have survived because they were incorporated into cemeteries. Other types of settings that were often "safe" for mounds include institutional grounds (e.g., the Fairmount and Poorhouse — now Shawnee Reservation — mounds), recreational areas (e.g., Moundbuilders Park), residences (e.g., Williams Mound), or relatively inaccessible locations (e.g., Norwood Mound, Glenford Fort) (Figure 15).

Most of the thousands of mounds and earthworks that were in the Ohio Valley, however, either have been destroyed or altered to the extent that their identity is lost to all but the most perceptive of observers. Agriculture, urban and industrial development, and the construction of transportation systems probably have been responsible for the destruction or alteration of most mounds or earthworks (Figures 5, 9). These activities have been prominent at such places as Athens, Charleston, Chillicothe, Cincinnati, Circleville, Columbus, Moundsville, and Newark, and in the fertile alluvial valleys of the Great Miami, Little Miami, Scioto, Licking, Hocking, Kanawha, and Ohio Rivers. Excavations by both curiosity seekers and professional

Figure 15. The Octagon Earthworks, Newark, Ohio, as they appeared late in the 1930s while managed as a golf course. This Hopewell geometric enclosure was part of an extensive mound and earthworks complex that spread over some 4 square miles. Notice that this feature is located on the second terrace above Raccoon Creek, visible at right. (Ohio Historical Society photograph.)

archeologists, too, altered or destroyed many mounds, especially during the 19th Century and early part of the 20th Century before modern methods and research objectives and legislative controls were implemented, and public awareness and concern were heightened. Natural and human-induced erosion has also taken its toll of mounds and earthworks.

The Myth of a Lost Race

While settlement spread through and increased in the Ohio Valley, differing ideas about the origin of the mounds and their builders arose and were discussed and investigated. Some of the earliest students of mounds, Thomas Jefferson among them, felt that the mounds found throughout the eastern United States were the work of American Indians. The size, complexity, and geometric precision of the Ohio Valley mounds and earthworks, however, led other people to believe that they were the product of some advanced civilization. Many people during the early part of the 19th Century believed strongly that the American Indian, as known by them, simply did not have the energy or organizational ability, or technological skills, to build the earthworks. In addition, there was romantic — perhaps nationalistic — appeal in the notion that a true civilization might have

27

existed in America prior to its discovery by the Europeans. Thus there arose a widespread feeling during the 19th Century that the mounds and earthworks had been built by a lost race of civilized people, but there was no consensus among the advocates of the lost race idea as to the identity of the people responsible. Vikings, Greeks, Israelites, Persians, Hindus, Phoenicians, and emigrants from Atlantis were all put forth as candidates. As to the fate of the Lost Race, it was believed that they either must have emigrated voluntarily — perhaps to Mexico to become the Toltecs — or were displaced or destroyed by the ancestors of the historic American Indians.

The notion of a Lost Race began to receive credible scientifically-based opposition near mid-century, notably from the banker, economist and physical anthropologist Albert Gallatin. Frederic Ward Putnam of Harvard University also was a strong voice against the Lost Race idea during the 1870s and 1880s. The scientifically based death-blow to the idea, however, came from the investigations of mound building cultures carried out by the Bureau of (American) Ethnology during the period 1882-1894. The summary opinion of the archeologists involved with this work was that the widespread prehistoric earthworks had indeed been built by American Indians, and by different cultural groups at that.

Major Studies of the Adena and Hopewell Mounds and Earthworks

Systematic investigations and descriptions of mounds, earthworks, and their contents began to appear during the early part of the 19th Century. These descriptions were important contributions to the increase and diffusion of knowledge at the time they were prepared, and some have retained importance because they document artifacts that have since been destroyed and they have come to occupy important places in the history of American archeology. Three regional studies conducted during the 19th Century were especially important.

Caleb Atwater, the postmaster at Circleville, Ohio, was commissioned to prepare a description of the Ohio Valley earthworks by the young American Antiquarian Society. Atwater's report, published in 1820 under the title *Description of the Antiquities Discovered in the State of Ohio and Other Western States,* was the first regional synthesis of an archeological subject and at the time was unparalleled in its degree of thoroughness.

A quarter century later, Ephriam George Squier, editor of *The Chillicothe Gazette,* and Dr. Edwin H. Davis, also of Chillicothe, were commissioned by the American Ethnological Society to conduct another, more extensive and thorough survey and investigation of the contents of the mounds in the eastern part of the Mississippi Valley. These men, with the assistance of Colonel Charles Whittlesey, formerly Surveyor General of the State of Ohio, and other antiquarians of the day investigated about 300 mounds and earthworks. Most of the earthworks and some of the mounds were surveyed and illustrated. (Some of the Squier and Davis illustrations are used in this book.) Approximately 200 mounds were also excavated before or during this survey. The report was published in 1848 by the Smithsonian Institution under the title *Ancient Monuments of the Mississippi Valley.* The artifacts from the mounds, however, were sold to William Blackmore, an Englishman, who eventually turned them over to the British Museum because no American institution had sufficient interest in the collection, or the money, to purchase it.

The third major study of mounds conducted during the 19th Century was that of the newly formed Bureau of Ethnology, created within the Smithsonian Institution in 1878 and placed under the direction of John Wesley Powell. In 1881, Powell put Cyrus Thomas in charge of the Bureau's archeology program and instructed him to investigate the nature of the mound builders in order to put to rest the matter of the identity of those people. Thomas sent several field teams into various parts of the eastern half of the United States to survey and excavate representative samples of mounds in the different regions. Several publications resulting from this work were issued during the course of the 12-year investigation with the summary report, *Report on the Mound Explorations of the Bureau of Ethnology,* being issued in 1894. This report described many mounds and their contents but it also revised many opinions about the identity and relationships of the mound building cultures and, in doing so, set the archeology of North American mound building cultures on a new course.

The study of mound builders after the Thomas report has dealt with identifying the cultural content of, and the relationships among, the different mound building groups. Study of the mound building cultures of the Ohio Valley during the last century has resulted in the recognition of several different mound building groups including the Adena and Hopewell. Other research questions have consisted of attempts to find chronological patterns within each of these groups, to document the lifeways of each group, and to determine the relationships among these groups and their antecedents, their contemporaries, and their followers. Workers such as Warren K. Moorehead, William C. Mills and Henry C. Shetrone were active during the early part of this period. More recently, workers central to the issues include, among others, Raymond S. Baby, David Brose, Don Dragoo, N'omi Greber, James B. Griffin, Martha Potter Otto, Olaf Prufer, Mark F. Seeman, and William S. Webb. The most current survey of Adena archeology is Don W. Dragoo, *Mounds for the Dead;* that for Hopewell archeology is David Brose and N'omi Greber (editors), *Hopewell Archaeology.* Although much progress has been made during the last 90 years toward better defining and understanding the Adena and Hopewell, much work still remains to be done on such basic questions as the origin, lifeways, interregional influence, and demise of these people.

Some Significant Consequences of the Study of Mounds

Investigations of mounds and earthworks have produced some note-worthy impacts on the development of American archeology and the protection and management of American antiquities. The first scientific excavation of an archeological site in the United States is attributed to Thomas Jefferson, who systematically excavated a mound in eastern Virginia in order to answer questions about the manner in which Indians were buried in mounds. General Rufus Putnam, a leader of the Marietta settlement, prepared what is considered the first map of archeological features when he platted the Marietta Earthworks. When large trees were being removed from upon the mounds in Marietta, the Reverend Manasseh Cutler, another leader of the Marietta settlement, counted the growth rings of these trees in order to approximate the minimum number of years that had transpired since the Marietta mounds were built. One tree yielded 463 rings, leading Cutler to conclude that the mounds could be no younger than the early 14th Century. This represented possibly the first recorded attempt to use tree ring dating to address an archeological problem. Caleb Atwater's description of the Ohio mounds is considered the first regional synthesis of an archeological problem in the United States, and his report was included in the first volume of the *Transactions and Collections of the American Antiquarian Society.* The Squier and Davis report in 1848 was the first scientific publication of the Smithsonian Institution, the principal institution supported by the United States government dealing with the study of natural history. The Mound Builder Survey directed by Cyrus Thomas was the first systematic project conducted by the Bureau of (American) Ethnology.

Largely through the efforts of Frederic Ward Putnam, curator of the Peabody Museum of Archaeology and Ethnology at Harvard University, Serpent Mound was saved from probable destruction. Eventually, this site was given to the Ohio State Archaeological and Historical Society by Harvard University to be used as a public park. The threat to Serpent Mound, made increasingly visible by Putnam's efforts, resulted in the Ohio Legislature passing, in 1888, the first antiquity law in the United States to protect archeological resources. When the ownership of Serpent Mound was transferred to the Ohio State Archaeological and Historical Society, it became one of the first archeological preserves in the United States to be managed for public visitation. This feature and adjacent mounds remain accessible to the public as a result of the Society's long term preservation and management efforts. Ohio's antiquity legislation and the creation of Serpent Mound park aroused nationwide interest in passing antiquities legislation and in preserving archeological sites for the enjoyment and enlightenment of the public.

SECTION II

MOUNDS AND EARTHWORKS
ACCESSIBLE TO THE PUBLIC

MOUNDS AND EARTHWORKS ACCESSIBLE TO THE PUBLIC

Forty-one mounds, earthworks, and affiliated sites are identified in this section (Figure 16, Table 2). Each site is described briefly. Detailed directions, information about public access and educational and recreational facilities, and one or more sources of additional information are provided for each site. The sites described in this section are arranged alphabetically.

Most of the sites listed here are managed to accommodate public visitation. Several of these provide interpretive facilities — ranging from museums to simple information signs — and other recreational opportunities, whereas other sites function primarily to preserve rather than interpret the mounds or earthworks. Tarleton Cross Mound, located near Tarleton, Ohio, recently has been closed to public use; we mention this fact because the mound is identified on state road maps as a point of interest, but we omit it from our guide because of its current accessibility status.

Some of the sites identified here are privately owned and not managed for public visitation; they are included because they have appeared recently on maps as points of interest. Most of these, however, can be seen easily from public roads. Permission should always be obtained from the landowner before entering upon private property.

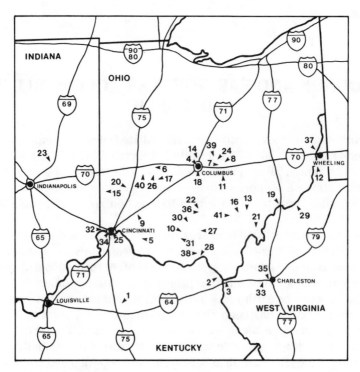

Figure 16. Publicly accessible mounds, earthworks and affiliated sites described in Section II
The numbered sites are identified in Table 2.

Table 2: Sites Described in Section II

1. Adena Park	21. Mound Cemetery
2. Ashland Central Park	22. Mound City Group National Monument
3. Camden Park Mound	23. Mounds State Park
4. Campbell Mound	24. Newark Earthworks
5. Elk Lick Road Mound	25. Norwood Mound
6. Enon Mound	26. Orator's Mound
7. Fairmount Mound	27. Piketon Mound Cemetery
8. Flint Ridge State Memorial	28. Portsmouth Mound Park
9. Fort Ancient State Memorial	29. Reynolds Mound
10. Fort Hill State Memorial	30. Seip Mound State Memorial
11. Glenford Fort	31. Serpent Mound State Memorial
12. Grave Creek Mound	32. Shawnee Lookout Park
13. Hartman Mound and	33. Shawnee Reservation Mound
Wolfe's Plains Group	34. Shorts Woods Park Mound
14. Highbanks Park Mound and Earthworks	35. South Charleston Mound
15. Hueston Woods Campground Mound	36. Story Mound
16. Indian Mound Campground	37. Tiltonsville Cemetery Mound
17. Indian Mound Park	38. Tremper Mound
18. Indian Mounds Park	39. Williams Mound
19. Marietta Earthworks	40. Wright Brothers Memorial Mound Group
20. Miamisburg Mound	41. Zaleski State Forest Mound

1. Adena Park

Adena earthworks
Fayette County, Kentucky

In the heart of the Bluegrass Region lies a prime example of the Ad "sacred circle" and one of the very few Adena monuments remaining in Kentucky. The enclosure at Adena Park has a diameter of 300' and an outside circumference of 750'. The embankment is 12'-14' wide at the base. The inner ditch, 12'-15' deep, has a midline circumference of 555'. A thirty three-foot wide opening in the embankment provides access via a causeway to an inner platform 150' in diameter. Both the causeway and the central area represent unexcavated portions of the original ground surface.

The Adena Park enclosure was part of a more extensive earthworks complex known as the Mt. Horeb Earthworks. One-half mile southwest of the circle was an elliptical embankment 3,900' long enclosing 25 acres. About .25 mile to the west was a low mound 3.5' high and about 70' in diameter. A circular work similar to the remaining enclosure but smaller (diameter = 125') was located 600' to the southwest.

The Mt. Horeb Earthworks — in particular, the sacred circle — caught the attention of early antiquarians and was described as early as 1824. The complex was surveyed in 1930, and the larger circle was proposed as a state park. In 1936, the site and 6 adjoining acres were purchased by private subscription and became the property of the Kentucky Archaeological Society. Today it is maintained as a park by the University of Kentucky for day use by its faculty, staff, and students and their families.

Excavations by the Works Progress Administration in 1939 revealed that a wooden structure once stood on the central platform. Paired post-holes formed a circle 97' in diameter. There was no obvious entrance and no evidence of there ever having been a roof. The structure's function is unknown, although William S. Webb, who directed the excavation, suggested it might have served as one clan's ceremonial and social center, somewhat like the circular, subterranean kivas of the Pueblo Indians of the American Southwest. Entry to the "open-air kiva" could have been gained by a ladder or a ramp over the posts.

DIRECTIONS: Exit Interstate 75 at Exit 115, go N on Kentucky Route 922 about 6 mi to Iron Works Pike, then E on Iron Works Pike .2 mi, then N on Mt. Horeb Pike 2.5 mi to Adena Park entrance on E side of road (Figure 17).

PUBLIC USE: Season and Hours: Open year round, by reservation, to students and employees of the University of Kentucky. Permission for persons not affiliated with the University to enter the park should be obtained from the Campus Recreation Department. Park closes at 10:00 PM. **Fees:** $10.00 deposit required to secure gate key. **Restrictions:** Driving or parking on the earthworks prohibited.

FOR ADDITIONAL INFORMATION: Contact: Campus Recreation Department, University of Kentucky, Seaton Building, Room 135, Lexington, KY 40506-0219, 606-257-2898. **Read:** Webb, W. S. 1941. Mt. Horeb earthworks, site 1 and the Drake Mound, site 11, Fayette County, Kentucky. University of Kentucky Papers in Anthropology and Archaeology, vol. 5, no. 2.

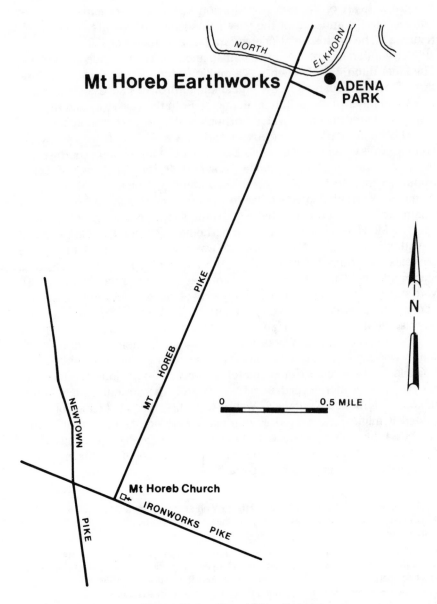

Figure 17. Location of Adena Park.

2. Ashland Central Park

(?)Burial mounds
Ashland, Boyd County, Kentucky

Located in the northwest part of Central Park is a string of six small mounds, each approximately 4'-5' high. These mounds have not been excavated by archeologists and consequently their cultural affiliation is not known.

DIRECTIONS: Follow U. S. Route 60 (12th Street) SW from U. S. Route 23 (Winchester Avenue) in downtown Ashland for about .4 mi (5 blocks from Winchester Avenue) to Lexington Avenue, then SE on Lexington Avenue .5 mi to park entrance on NE side of street. Parking is available in park (Figure 18).

PUBLIC USE: Season and Hours: The park is open daily throughout the year during daylight hours. **Recreation facilities:** Picnic area, restrooms, playground, game fields, exercise course.

FOR ADDITIONAL INFORMATION: Contact: Parks and Recreation Department, City of Ashland, Ashland, KY 41101, 606-325-8571.

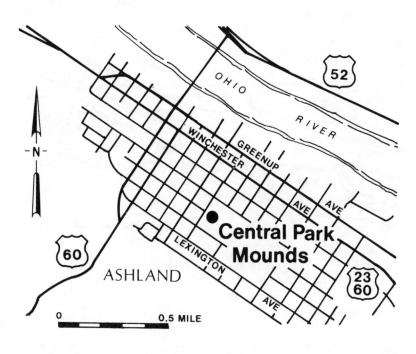

Figure 18. Location of Ashland Central Park.

37

3. Camden Park Mound

(?)Adena burial mound
Wayne County, West Virginia

The Camden Park Mound, a conical mound perhaps 20' high, is located near the center of the Camden Amusement Park, just west of Huntington, West Virginia. This feature is located on the Ohio River floodplain; its shape, size and location suggest that it is an Adena burial mound. This mound is fenced.

DIRECTIONS: Take Exit 6 from Interstate 64 onto U.S. 52. The first right ramp onto Madison Avenue leads to the front gate of the park. Parking is available inside the park (Figure 19).

PUBLIC USE: Season and hours: 10:00 AM-10:00 PM, Sunday through Friday, 10:00 AM through 11:00 PM, Saturday, last week of April through Labor Day. Open weekends only in April and September. **Fees:** Admission to the amusement park is $0.25.

FOR ADDITIONAL INFORMATION: Contact: Camden Park, P.O. Box 9245, Huntington, WV 25104, 304-429-4231.

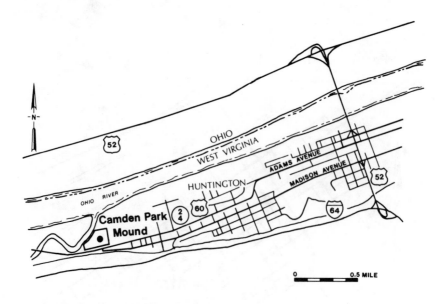

Figure 19. Location of Camden Park.

4. Campbell Mound

Adena burial mound
Columbus, Franklin County, Ohio

Campbell Mound, one of the few remaining Adena burial mounds in Columbus, is a flat-topped conical feature measuring 20' high and 100' in diameter at the base. The mound is situated in the center of a small tract of land approximately 1 acre in size that is owned and maintained by the Ohio Historical Society as a public roadside park. A stone wall extends along the front, or road, side of this park. A circular path leads to the top of the mound, from which an adjacent limestone quarry can be seen. The mound site is completely surrounded by disturbed terrain, documenting the conscious effort made to preserve this feature.

The park containing Campbell Mound is small and undesignated; no signs direct you to the site or tell you when you have arrived. Vegetation along the road in this semi-developed area obscures the site until you are nearly upon it. Our suggestion is to drive slowly, traffic (which is sometimes heavy) permitting, and be prepared to pull off the pavement along side the stone wall when it comes into view. This wall extends along the edge of the site and is more easily seen from a moving car than is the mound itself.

DIRECTIONS: Exit Interstate 70 at Exit 94 (Wilson Road), go N on Wilson Road about 1 mi to Trabue Road, then east on Trabue Road about 1.6 mi to McKinley Avenue (at 2nd set of traffic lights on Trabue Road — do not cross multiple railroad tracks), then S on McKinley Avenue .5 mi to Campbell Mound on W side of street. Roadside parking on W side of McKinley Avenue (Figure 20).

PUBLIC USE: Season and Hours: Open year round during daylight hours. **Fees:** none.

FOR ADDITIONAL INFORMATION: Contact: Ohio Historical Society, 1985 Velma Avenue, Columbus, OH 43211, 614-466-1500.

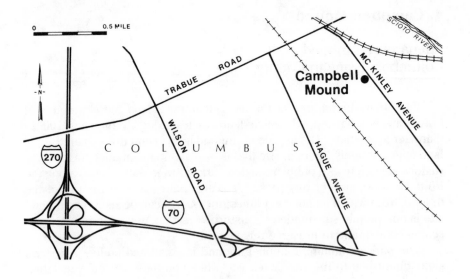

Figure 20. Location of Campbell Mound.

5. Elk Lick Road Mound

(?)Adena burial mound
Clermont County, Ohio

The Elk Lick Road Mound is located in a fenced enclosure in the picnic grounds in the southern part of East Fork State Park. The small, conical mound is approximately 5' high and 50' in diameter. This feature has never been excavated, but it is presumed to be an Adena burial mound because of its conical shape and upland location.

DIRECTIONS: From Ohio Route 125 at Bantam, go N into East Fork State Park on Park Road 1 for about 1 mi, then W on Park Road 2 for about 500', then N into picnic area (Figure 21).

PUBLIC USE: Season and hours: The park is open year round during daylight hours.

FOR ADDITIONAL INFORMATION: Contact: Division of State Parks, Ohio Department of Natural Resources, Fountain Square, Columbus, OH 43211, 614-265-7000.

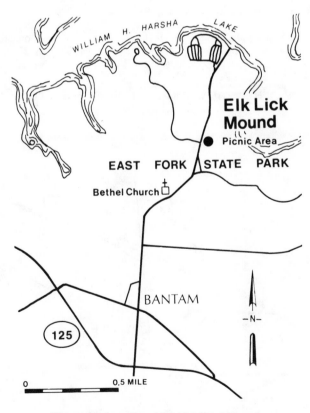

Figure 21. Location of Elk Lick Road Mound.

41

6. Enon Mound

Adena burial mound
Enon, Clark County, Ohio

This well preserved 40' high conical mound, also known as Knob Prairie Mound, is said to be the second largest Adena mound in Ohio. Only the Miamisburg Mound is higher. With a basal circumference of 574', the Enon Mound contains an estimated 12,800 cubic yards of earth. The mound is fenced.

It is not known for certain that Enon Mound has ever been excavated. An unsubstantiated report suggests that the interior of the mound was explored by local citizens in the 1870s. According to the story, a vertical shaft sunk from top center uncovered an oven-shaped room made of stone at the center of which was an altar with animal bones and charcoal. There is no indication of human burials or artifacts having been found.

Another unsubstantiated story says that George Rogers Clark scanned the horizon from the mound in 1780 prior to his attack on the Shawnee village of Picawey about 2 miles to the north.

DIRECTIONS: Exit Interstate 70 at Exit 48 (via Ohio Route 4 if eastbound) onto Enon Road, go S 1 mi to Enon, then NE on Main Street .3 mi, then SE on Indian Drive for 250' to the mound. Mound Circle, a street around the mound, is one-way to the right. Curbside parking is available on Mound Circle (Figure 22).

FOR ADDITIONAL INFORMATION: Contact: Enon Historical Society, P.O. Box 442, Enon, OH 45323.

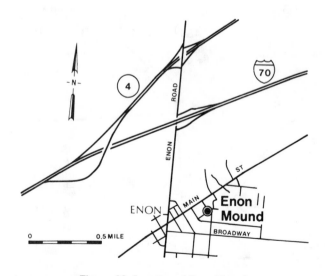

Figure 22. Location of Enon Mound.

7. Fairmount Mound

Adena burial mound
Licking County, Ohio

The privately owned Fairmount Mound, located on the grounds of the Fairmount Presbyterian Church, is a flat topped conical feature approximately 15' high and 80' in diameter at the base. This is one of the few large burial mounds remaining in Licking County. The mound is mowed periodically, but normally is covered with low growing vegetation. The mound is located on a ridgecrest overlooking the scenic rolling hills of the western Appalachian Plateau.

DIRECTIONS: Exit Interstate 70 at Ohio Route 13 (Jacksontown Interchange), go N on Route 13 about 1 mi to U.S. Route 40, then E on Route 40 for 1.5 mi, then N on Licking County Route 323 (Fairmount Road) .15 mi to crest of ridge. Mound is easily seen at crest of ridge to E of red brick Fairmount Church. Parking available at church (Figure 23).

PUBLIC USE: Restrictions: Fairmount Mound is privately owned. Permission should be obtained from the landowner before entering upon the property.

FOR ADDITIONAL INFORMATION: Contact: Fairmount Presbyterian Church, Jacksontown, OH 43030.

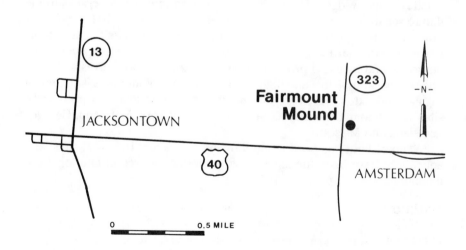

Figure 23. Location of Fairmount Mound.

8. Flint Ridge State Memorial

Prehistoric flint quarry
Licking County, Ohio

Flint Ridge State Memorial is a 525 acre cultural and natural preserve created in 1933 to preserve part of a significant natural area and prehistoric flint quarry. Flint Ridge is a natural elongate chain of narrow hills extending roughly east-west for about seven miles through the eastern part of Licking and the western part of Muskingum counties. The ridge has formed where pockets or beds of resistant Vanport Flint have been exposed by erosion. Deposits of the Vanport Flint range from a few inches to several feet in thickness along the ridge, but average 1'-5'. Near Flint Ridge State Memorial, however, the deposits reach 12' in thickness. The gem quality flint is translucent and variously colored, including white, yellow, pink, salmon, red, blue, green and black. The different colors are caused by iron or other inorganic impurities.

The Vanport Flint outcrops along Flint Ridge constitute one of the most extensive surface deposits of high-quality flint in the eastern part of the United States. As a result, this material was exploited by Indians from the Paleo-Indian period up into the early historic period, as well as by the Anglo-Americans who settled the Muskingum Valley. The surface of the ridge is pitted from thousands of years of human activity. The weathered surface exposures of flint were of little or no value for use as tools, so prehistoric peoples had to quarry the deeper, unweathered subsurface deposits. This quarrying was done with heavy stone or wooden hammers and wood or bone wedges. The wedges were driven into natural cracks in the flint to separate large blocks. These were then reduced in size for transport away from the quarry or were worked into tools at the site. Most tools made from the hard flint were for cutting, scraping, drilling or puncturing purposes, and included projectile points, scrapers, drills, knives and awls. The relative abundance and high quality of Vanport Flint made it an item of regular and extensive trade; the material has been found in prehistoric sites throughout Ohio and as far away as New York, Maryland, Georgia, Louisiana and Missouri.

Vanport Flint has been found in many Adena and Hopewell sites, and appears to have been the single most important source of flint for these moundbuilding peoples.

DIRECTIONS: Exit Interstate 70 onto Ohio Route 668 (Brownsville Exit), go N on Route 668 about 3.75 mi to Flint Ridge State Memorial on E side of road, at crest of ridge (Figure 24).

PUBLIC USE: Season and hours: The Memorial grounds are open 9:30 AM-5:00 PM, Wednesday through Saturday, Noon-5:00 PM Sundays and holidays, Memorial Day through Labor Day; same hours, weekends only, Labor Day through October. Closed November through Memorial Day. **Fees:** None. **Recreational facilities:** Picnic area, restrooms, hiking,

44

birding. **Handicapped facilities:** Of special significance at Flint Ridge State Memorial is a 1,100' long nature trail for handicapped persons. The trail is paved and has a hand rail. Interpretive signs are in Braille as well as printed in English. This award winning facility was the first of its kind in the state. **Restrictions:** Flint must not be removed from the Memorial grounds.

EDUCATIONAL FACILITIES: Museum: The Memorial museum, constructed in 1968, depicts the geological and human history of Flint Ridge. Central among the exhibits is a life-sized diorama depicting Indians quarrying flint from an authentic quarry pit, over and around which the museum was built. Other exhibits describe the formation and distribution of flint, Ohio's official gemstone, at Flint Ridge and elsewhere in Ohio; flint-working techniques and the products produced; and the distribution of flint as a trade item across the eastern U.S. **Museum hours:** Same as grounds hours (above). **Fees:** Admission $1.50 adults, $1.00 children 6-12. **Bookstore:** The museum has a small selection of books on archeology and natural history, along with other educational materials. **Trails:** Two nature trails (.5 mi and 2 mi) extend through the wooded nature reserve, providing access to the upland forest, the ridge itself, aboriginal quarries and outcrops of flint.

FOR ADDITIONAL INFORMATION: Contact: Ohio Historical Society, 1985 Velma Avenue, Columbus, OH 43211, 614-466-1500. **Read:** (1) DeLong, R. M. 1972. Bedrock geology of the Flint Ridge area, Licking and Muskingum Counties, Ohio. Ohio Division of Geological Survey Report of Investigations no. 95. (2) Stout, W., and R. A. Schoenlach. 1945. The occurrence of Flint in Ohio. Ohio Division of Geological Survey, fourth series — Bulletin 46.

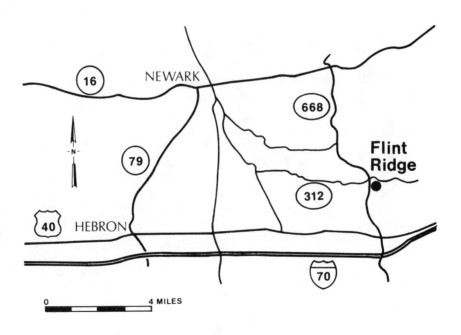

Figure 24. Location of Flint Ridge State Memorial.

45

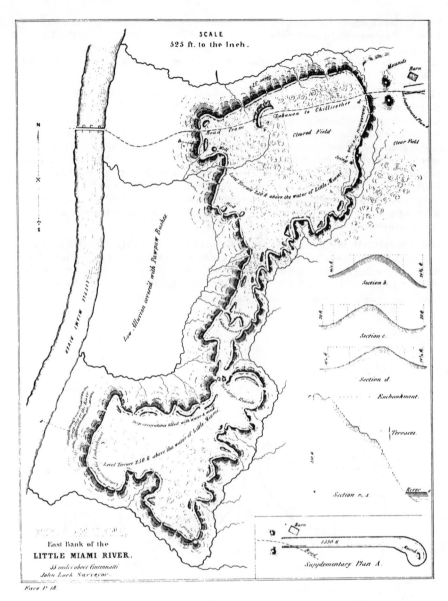

Figure 25. Fort Ancient as depicted in Squier and Davis, 1848.

9. Fort Ancient State Memorial

Hopewell hilltop enclosure
Warren County, Ohio

Fort Ancient, Ohio's first state park (1891), preserves an outstanding example of the Hopewell hilltop enclosure (Figure 25). The fort is easily accessible and readily visible. Fort Ancient has long been recognized as one of the most important prehistoric sites in the United States and was occupied by both the Hopewell and the later Fort Ancient Culture (A.D. 1000-1650) of the Mississippian Period.

Typical of hilltop enclosures, Fort Ancient lies on a nearly isolated promontory, set off from most of the main surface by steep ravines. Situated 275' above the Little Miami River, the earthen and stone walls wind 3.5 miles around the perimeter of the hilltop. (The irregular outline was once interpreted as a map of the Americas, North, Central and South!) The walls, now restored, vary in height from 4' to 33.5', the highest segment being in the northeast where an isolating ravine is absent and the promontory is connected with the more extensive upland surface. Where the hillside is exceptionally steep, there is no wall at all.

Fort Ancient is divided into the North, Middle and South Forts. In all, 100 acres are enclosed. The maximum length from north to south is 4,993' or over .9 mile. Mounds and other earthworks are located inside and outside the walls.

DIRECTIONS: From Columbus, follow Interstate 71 S to Exit 36, exit onto Warren County Route 7, go E about .25 mi to Warren County Route 45, then S on Route 45 about 2 mi to intersection with Ohio Route 350, then W on Route 350 about 1 mi to park entrance. From Cincinnati, follow Interstate 71 N to Exit 32, exit onto Ohio Route 123, go SE on Route 123 for several hundred feet, then E (first left) on Route 350 for 3 mi to Fort Ancient (Figure 26).

PUBLIC USE: Season and Hours: The Memorial grounds are open 9:30 AM-5:00 PM, Wednesday through Saturday, Noon-5:00 PM, Sunday and holidays, Memorial Day through Labor Day; same hours, weekends only, Labor Day through October. Closed November through Memorial Day. **Fees:** Admission $2.00 per car to enter park. **Recreational facilities:** Picnic areas, restrooms, hiking. **Restrictions:** Climbing on mounds is not permitted. Pets must be on leash. Alcoholic beverages are not permitted.

EDUCATIONAL FACILITIES: Museum: Aspects of Hopewell ceremonial life are depicted in exhibits which model a shaman, a charnel house, and a cross-section of a burial mound. Hopewell art and craftsmanship are displayed. A relief map, to scale, of Fort Ancient is on view. Exhibits dealing with the archeology of the Fort Ancient Culture are also presented. **Museum hours:** Same as grounds hours (above). **Fees:** Park entry fee includes admission to museum. **Bookstore:** The museum gift shop offers a modest selection of books on archeology and natural history subjects, as well as other educational materials. **Trails:** Interpretative trails lead to segments of the fort and two overlooks. A connector trail descends the bluff to the Little Miami River.

FOR ADDITIONAL INFORMATION: Contact: Ohio Historical Society, 1985 Velma Avenue, Columbus, OH 43211, 614-466-1500. **Read:** Morgan, R. C. 1970. Fort Ancient. Columbus: Ohio Historical Society.

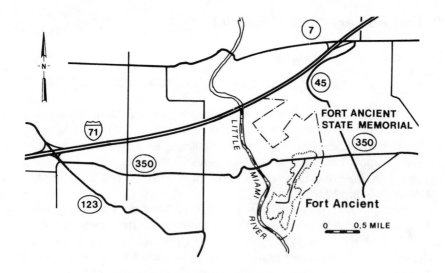

Figure 26. Location of Fort Ancient.

10. Fort Hill State Memorial

Hopewell hilltop enclosure
Highland County, Ohio

Fort Hill is the only major Ohio Hopewell earthworks managed for public visitation that has not been restored. The earthen and stone walls are overgrown with trees and vines, providing an appearance similar to that first viewed by settlers in the 19th Century. A rather steep trail leads up to the fort, which is situated 500' above Ohio Brush Creek on an isolated hilltop — part of the deeply eroded western edge of the Appalachian Plateau. Like all of the Hopewell forts, the walls of Fort Hill follow the irregular contour of the hilltop. About 1.6 miles in total length, the walls are 6'-15' high and 45' wide at the base. There are 33 irregularly spaced openings, each about 20' wide. The fort walls enclose about 48 acres (Figure 27).

Three large structures — two circular and one rectangular — have been discovered at the base of the hill. These buildings suggest to some archeologists that the fort was used for ceremonial rather than defense purposes. One of the circular structures had a diameter of 175' and may have been an arbor covering living sites. The rectangular building, of double post construction, may have been a workshop area. Measuring 120' × 80', it represents the largest Hopewell building discovered.

Fort Hill is located on a 1,200 acre nature preserve. The park lies at the junction of several natural regions, each with a distinctive physiography, geology and Ice Age history. This environmental diversity results in an unusual variety of native plants and animals in this region. Fort Hill is as significant for its natural history as for its human prehistory.

DIRECTIONS: From U.S.50, go S on Ohio Route 41 about 11 mi, then W on Fort Hill Road .75 mi to park entrance on S side of road. Parking available at museum and picnic area (Figure 28).

PUBLIC USE: Season and Hours: The Memorial grounds are open 9:30 AM-5:00 PM, Wednesday through Saturday, Noon-5:00 PM, Sunday and holidays, Memorial Day through Labor Day; same hours, weekends only, Labor Day through October. Closed November through Memorial Day. **Fees:** None. **Recreational facilities:** Picnic area, restrooms, hiking, birding. **Restrictions:** Pets must be on leash. Bikes and motorbikes allowed on roadways only. Alcoholic beverages not permitted.

EDUCATIONAL FACILITIES: Museum: Natural history and Hopewell archeology are featured in the museum. There are models of the circular and rectangular structures excavated at the base of the hill, and an exhibit on the geology of Ohio. **Museum hours:** Same as grounds hours (above). **Fees:** None. **Trails:** Over 10 miles of trails traverse the park. The Fort Trail (2 miles) goes up to the fort, over the walls, and along the full length of the enclosure. Gorge Trail and Deer Trail (4 and 5 miles, respectively) circle the base of Fort Hill.

FOR ADDITIONAL INFORMATION: Contact: Ohio Historical Society, 1985 Velma Road, Columbus, OH 43211, 614-466-1500. **Read:** Morgan, R. G., and E. S. Thomas. 1948. Fort Hill. Columbus: Ohio State Archaeological and Historical Society.

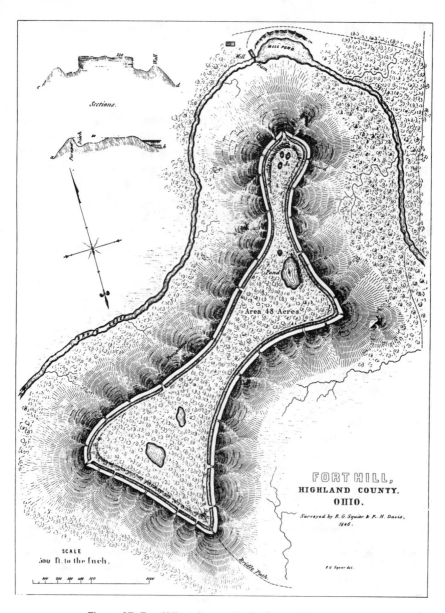

Figure 27. Fort Hill as depicted in Squier and Davis, 1848.

50

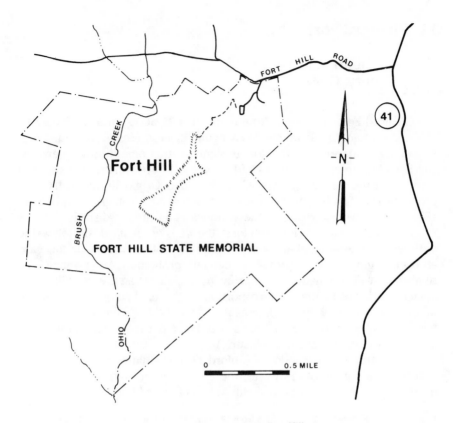

Figure 28. Location of Fort Hill.

11. Glenford Fort

Hopewell hilltop enclosure
Perry County, Ohio

Glenford Fort encloses a little more than 27 acres on a ridgetop 200′ above Jonathan Creek in the Muskingum River drainage system. Unrestored and undeveloped, this fort is significant as one of only a very few surviving hilltop enclosures. Its 6,610′ long walls are constructed solely of stone from the sandstone caprock of the ridge. Originally the walls were probably 7′-20′ in height, but today average 1′ to 1.5′ high. Even back in 1820, Caleb Atwater wrote, "...these stones lie in utmost disorder."

In common with all Hopewell forts, the walls of Glenford Fort follow the outline of the hilltop and are absent where natural defenses — in this case an overhanging ledge — provided adequate protection. An entrance with re-entrant walls opened onto a narrow neck connecting the fort hill to the adjacent upland. In the western portion of the enclosure stood a stone mound described by Cyrus Thomas in 1894 as 12′ high and 100′ in diameter. (In Atwater's earlier, but highly stylized map of the site, this mound was placed in the center of the enclosure.)

In its stone construction, Glenford Fort is unique among the forts described in this book. However, there were other stone forts, perhaps most notable the one at Spruce Hill in Ross County, Ohio.

DIRECTIONS: Follow Ohio Route 757 S from Glenford about .5 mi, then E on Township Road 19 for .2 mi to the Cooperrider farm. The fort is reached by a primitive footpath (Figure 29).

PUBLIC USE: Restrictions: This is an undeveloped site on private property. Visitors are requested to ask permission from the landowner before visiting the fort.

FOR ADDITIONAL INFORMATION: Contact: The Don Cooperrider Family, 4265 Twp Rd. 19, N.W., Glenford, OH 43739.

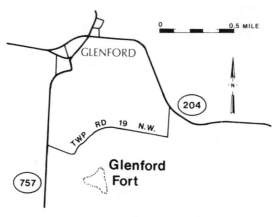

Figure 29. Location of Glenford Fort.

52

12. Grave Creek Mound

Adena burial mound
Moundsville, Marshall County, West Virginia

The Grave Creek Mound is the most important prehistoric monument in West Virginia. Together with the Adena mound in Miamisburg, Ohio, these are the largest prehistoric burial mounds in the Ohio Valley. Originally 65' high, the summit of Grave Creek Mound today rises 62' above the surface of the Moundsville Bottoms on the second terrace of Grave Creek. With a basal diameter of 240', the mound is formed of an estimated 57,000 tons of earth — the equivalent of 3,000,000 basket loads. Earth for the mound came from an encircling moat. The moat, with its one causeway, was obliterated after excavations in 1838. Scientific testing in 1975-76 substantiated its existence and determined that it had been 40' wide, 4'-5' deep and had had a midline circumference of 910'.

The Grave Creek Mound is the only remaining feature of what was an important and impressive Adena and Hopewell mound and earthworks complex (Figure 30). North of the mound was an octagon that enclosed about 5 acres. Smaller mounds surrounded the "Mammoth Mound", as Grave Creek was called in the 19th and early part of the 20th centuries. A graded way similar to the *Sacra Via* in Marietta, Ohio, led from the large mound to the Ohio River. Two smaller earthworks described as forts were reported in existence in 1785. The Grave Creek complex was one of a series of Adena mounds and Hopewell earthworks which lined this section of the Ohio River on the West Virginia side. The others have been obliterated entirely.

Excavations of the great mound have revealed several burials at different levels; at least two were Adena, one was probably Hopewell, and others are Late Woodland intrusive burials. Various Adena artifacts plus a highly controversial inscribed sandstone tablet have been reported from this site. (The tablet has 22 characters resembling the Old Phoenician alphabet and 1 ideograph. Its authenticity is disputed.) Adena occupation of the area extended from the 3rd Century B.C. to the 2nd Century A.D.

Since its discovery by early settlers in 1770, the Grave Creek Mound has had a varied history. At one time a museum was built inside it. Later a saloon was erected on top, and still later the mound became the site of the Marshall County fair. Around its base ran a racetrack — a use to which mounds and enclosures have been put frequently throughout the region occupied by the Adena and Ohio Hopewell. In 1909, the State of West Virginia acquired the great mound, and its maintenance was directed by the Superintendent of the State Penitentiary, which is located across the street east of the mound. Since 1967 it has been the centerpiece of a state park. Stone steps lead to the top of the mound.

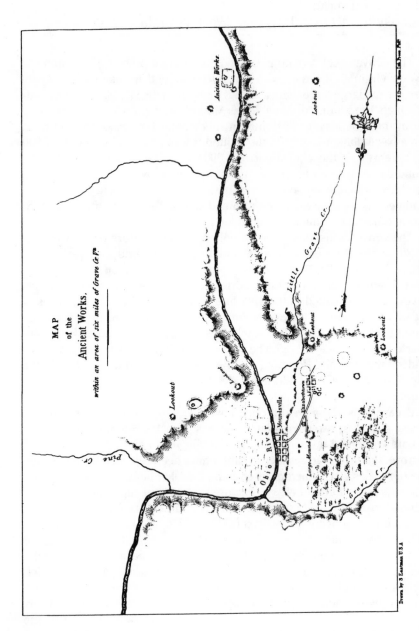

Figure 30. Grave Creek Earthworks as depicted in Schoolcraft, 1851. The "Large Mound" is Grave Creek Mound.

DIRECTIONS: From West Virginia Route 2 in Moundsville, go E on 8th Street 1 block to Grave Creek State Park. Entry to the mound site is through the Delf Norona Museum and Cultural Centre. Parking is available on the E (Jefferson Avenue) side of the park grounds (Figure 31).

PUBLIC USE: Season and Hours: 10:00 AM-4:30 PM, Monday through Saturday; Noon-5:00 PM, Sundays. **Fees:** None. **Food service:** The Mound Museum Restaurant offers lunch from 11:00 AM-2:00 PM, Tuesday through Friday. **Recreational facilities:** Picnic area, restrooms. **Handicapped facilities:** A wheelchair ramp provides access to the mound area. Wheelchairs are available for public use. **Restrictions:** Pets are not allowed.

EDUCATIONAL FACILITIES: Museum: The Delf Norona Museum and Cultural Centre exhibits include an overview of archeology in West Virginia; the discovery, uses, and excavations of the Grave Creek or Mammoth Mound by Americans; and the Adena culture. A diorama shows the mound under construction. A participatory exhibit "for kids by kids" is being developed to demonstrate a cave, a quarry, a mound and an archeological excavation. **Fees:** Admission to the museum exhibits is $1.00 for adults, $.50 for children (6-18). **Bookstore:** The museum gift shop has a modest selection of books and other publications dealing with archeology and natural history, along with other types of educational materials. **Special group activities:** The museum will provide special lectures to groups, but arrangements must be made in advance.

FOR ADDITIONAL INFORMATION: Contact: Delf Norona Museum and Cultural Centre, 801 Jefferson Avenue, Moundsville, WV 26041, 304-843-1410. **Read:** (1) Norona, Delf. 1962. Moundsville's Mammoth Mound. Special Publication of the West Virginia Archeological Society, No. 6. (2) Hemmings, E. T. 1984. "Fairchance Mound and village: An Early Middle Woodland settlement in the Upper Ohio Valley." West Virginia Archeologist, vol. 36, no. 1, pp. 3-68 (including two appendices). (3) Hemmings, E. T. 1984. Investigations at Grave Creek Mound 1975-76: a sequence for mound and moat construction. West Virginia Archeologist, vol. 36, no. 2, pp. 3-49.

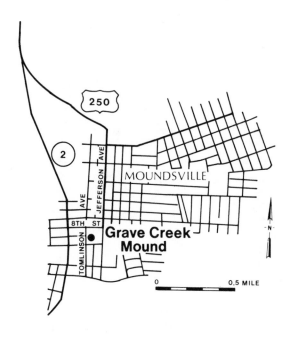

Figure 31. Location of Grave Creek Mound.

55

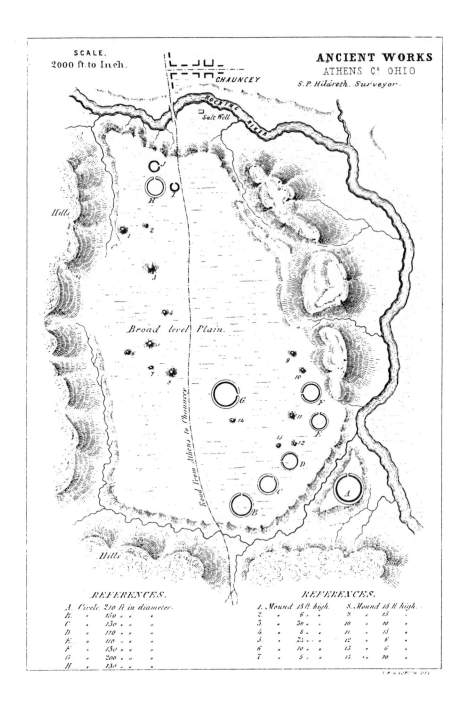

Figure 32. Wolfe's Plains Earthworks as depicted in Squier and Davis, 1848. Although this illustration clearly shows the general pattern of mound distribution across the level surface, some of the individual features were not located accurately.

56

13. Hartman Mound and the Wolfe's Plains Group

Adena burial mounds and sacred circles
The Plains, Athens County, Ohio

Within the hilly uplands of the western Appalachian Plateau, in the valley of the Hocking River, is a relatively level surface encompassing some 4 or 5 square miles. This surface, known as Wolfe's Plains and The Plains, was formed by the deposition of glacial outwash sediments carried away from the glacial front by meltwater during the Illinoian or Wisconsinan glaciation. Such broad expanses of level ground are rare in the unglaciated parts of Ohio. Between 300 B.C. and A. D. 200, The Plains were exploited by the Adena Indians, who built here one of their largest concentrations of burial mounds and sacred circles (Figure 32). (The greatest cluster of Adena mounds and enclosures was in the Scioto Valley near Chillicothe, Ohio, and the second largest group was near Charleston, West Virginia. The Plains group is the third largest.) At least two dozen burial mounds and eight sacred circles are known to have existed on Wolfe's Plains, but, as elsewhere, most of these features have been destroyed, and the survivors are disappearing. Those that remain are in various stages of preservation and provide a record of the nature of this important complex as well as — instructively — the processes that continue to reduce it. Six burial mounds and one sacred circle remain wholly or partially intact within the village of The Plains. At least three other mounds and one sacred circle are known in surrounding areas.

The largest and best preserved of the Wolfe's Plains Group is the Hartman Mound, also known as the George Connett Mound. This mound is 40' high and 140' in diameter at the base. It has never been excavated. A smaller mound about 6' high was once located near the Hartman mound. It was excavated by Andrews, who in 1875-76 headed the first survey of archeological sites in the Hocking Valley. In it he discovered a log tomb with a skeleton surrounded by 500 rolled copper beads. There was also a copper tubular block-ended pipe in this smaller of the George Connett Mounds, the only such object found in an Adena burial. The surviving Hartman Mound is situated on a small privately owned tract of land within the Adena Park housing development and is bordered on two sides by roads.

A second well preserved mound is the largest of what was a cluster of three mounds called the Woodruff Connett Mounds. This conical mound is 15' high and 90' in diameter at the base. The second largest of the group was 6' high and 40' in diameter; it is now discernible as a swell in the ground. The third has been destroyed completely. A park has been proposed to save the two remaining mounds from further destruction, but they have not yet been afforded this protection.

Dorr Mound 1, reported by Squier and Davis to have been 15' high, is presently cultivated as part of a cornfield; while Dorr Mound 2 (10' high according to Squier and Davis's survey) is within a fenced chicken yard. Both of these mounds have been excavated, but no reports of findings exist.

The Martin Mound 2 is a small crescent-shaped mound that was excavated and produced a child's skeleton. This feature is discernible from West First Street. The Martin Mound 1 was 18' high before most of it was leveled in 1875 to provide an elevated site for a schoolhouse. Excavation caused excitement among the village residents when a piece of buckskin clothing covered with copper beads was discovered. The dress was torn in pieces so everyone could have a sample. A residence whose base is slightly but noticeably higher than adjacent buildings now occupies the site of Martin Mound 1 on the west side of Route 682 between West First Street and Connett Road.

The Armitage Mound was originally 7' high and 100' in diameter. It is reduced in size today as a result of long agricultural use.

Among the mounds of The Plains that have been destroyed was the large Beard (Baird, or Coon) Mound, whose excavation by Emerson Greenman resulted in one of the first treatises on Adena culture. This mound was 30' high and 114' in diameter at the base. It is the only Adena mound in Ohio known to have contained mica, a material more frequently associated with the Hopewell culture. The mound was subsequently destroyed by road building; its site is occupied, in part, by The Plains volunteer fire department.

DIRECTIONS: Exit U. S. Route 33 at Ohio Route 682 (The Plains exit), go S on Route 682 about .25 mi into The Plains to Mound Street, then W on Mound Street about .1 mi to Hartman Mound, located immediately N of Mound Street. Figure 33 shows the location of other burial mounds and sacred circles in The Plains. Each of the features is identified by a roadside sign.

PUBLIC USE: Season and hours: All of the extant mounds and circles can be viewed from public roads throughout the year. **Restrictions:** All of the extant mounds and sacred circles are on private property. Permission should be obtained from the landowner before entering any site.

EDUCATIONAL FACILITIES: Special events: In an effort to elevate public awareness and appreciation of the mound resources of Wolfe's Plains, and to encourage preservation of the remaining features, a civic group in The Plains sponsors an annual Indian Mound Festival. This event, which features tours of the mound sites, is held the first full weekend (Saturday and Sunday) in October.

FOR ADDITIONAL INFORMATION: Contact: Ohio Historical Society, 1985 Velma Avenue, Columbus, OH 43211, 614-466-1500. **Read:** (1) Greenman, E. C. 1932. Excavation of the Coon Mound and an analysis of the Adena Culture. Ohio State Archaeological and Historical Quarterly, vol. 41, pp. 366-523. (2) Murphy, J. L. 1975. An archeological history of the Hocking Valley. Ohio University Press.

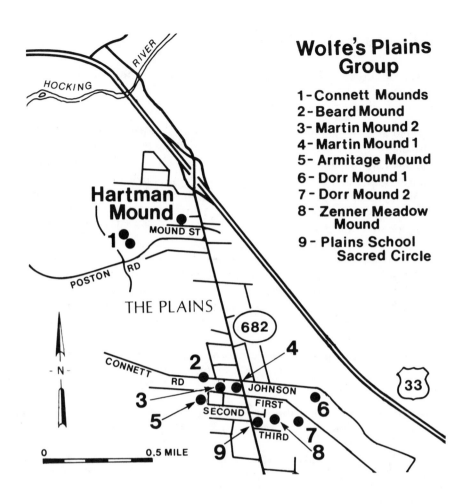

Figure 33. Location of Hartman Mound and other of the Wolfe's Plains Group.

14. Highbanks Park Earthworks

Adena burial mound and (?)Late Woodland earthworks
Delaware County, Ohio

Highbanks Park Mound II (Orchard Mound; Selvey Mound) and the Highbanks Park Earthworks are located east of the Olentangy River in the Highbanks Metro Park. Mound II is a small, subconical earthen burial mound about 2.5' high and 45' in diameter. Although unexcavated, this mound is presumed to be Adena because of its shape and upland location.

The Highbanks Park Works is a semi-elliptical earthen blufftop fortification located at the top of a 100' cliff overlooking the Olentangy River to the west. A ditch borders the exterior of the embankment to the east and north. The walls of the embankments are about 3' high. The depth of the exterior ditch varies from 3'-7'. Three openings, probably gateways, occur in the embankment. This earthwork is considered to represent a protective or defensive feature associated with a settlement of Late Woodland — possibly Cole — Indians; the feature was probably constructed between A.D. 800 and A.D. 1300.

Both Mound II and the bluff-top fortification are reached by the Overlook Trail (approximately 2.8 miles round trip) which begins near the east end of the picnic area.

DIRECTIONS: Highbanks Metro Park is located on the W side of U. S. Route 23, about 4 mi N of the Route 23-Interstate 270 interchange north of Columbus. Signs identify the entrance to the park (Figure 34).

PUBLIC USE: Season and hours: Open daily 7:00 AM until dark, year round. **Restrictions:** Visitors must remain on improved trails. Natural features may not be disturbed. Pets must be on leash and are confined to the picnic areas, parking areas, or roadways. Alcoholic beverages are not permitted.

FOR ADDITIONAL INFORMATION: Contact: Metropolitan Park District of Columbus and Franklin County, P. O. 29169, Columbus, OH 43229, 614-891-0700.

Figure 34. Location of the Highbanks Mound and Earthworks.

15. Hueston Woods Campground Mound

(?)Adena burial mound
Preble County, Ohio

This single conical mound, approximately 15' high, lies about 100 yards west of Row B in the Class A camping section of the Hueston Woods State Park campground. The feature has not been excavated so its actual cultural affiliation is not known, but it is similar in size and configuration to other Adena burial mounds. The mound is located in a grove of old beech trees on a narrow terrace between two tributaries of Four Mile Creek. A log fence encloses the feature. The mound is reached by walking along a mowed pathway. The 200 acre beech forest in Hueston Woods State Park has been designated a National Natural Landmark.

DIRECTIONS: Follow U. S. Route 27 to Oxford, then go N on Ohio Route 732 about 5 mi to park entrance. Signs along road provide direction to park, and signs in park provide direction to campground. There is no established parking area near the mound. Visitors wishing to see the mound must park either along the road at the end of Row B or elsewhere and walk to the mound (Figure 35).

PUBLIC USE: Season and Hours: The park and campground are open year round; grounds close to non-campers at 11:00 PM. **Fees:** No entrance fees. Fees are charged for the use of some of the Park's facilities. **Recreational facilities:** Include picnic area, restrooms, camping, horseback riding, hiking, water sports, winter sports.

FOR ADDITIONAL INFORMATION: Contact: Division of State Parks, Ohio Department of Natural Resources, Fountain Square, Columbus, OH 43211, 614-265-7000.

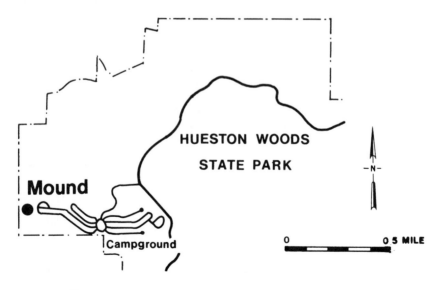

Figure 35. Location of the Hueston Woods Campground Mound.

16. Indian Mound Campground

Adena burial mound
Athens County, Ohio

This conical Adena burial mound is located in a commercial campground in the picturesque Hocking Valley of southeastern Ohio. The mound, now approximately 7' high, is situated near the top of a ridge within a nearly level field which was planted in corn for several years. The mound is now grass-covered and mowed, and its shape, somewhat flattened by tilling, is easily discernible. The mound was excavated in 1940, at which time one complete human skeleton in the extended burial position and various artifacts were located.

DIRECTIONS: Exit U. S. Route 33 onto Ohio State Route 682 either NW of Athens (if southbound) or in S Athens (if northbound). Take Route 682 to Ohio Route 56, go W on Route 56 to Athens County Route 6, then go S on Route 6 through the community of New Marshfield to Athens County Route 8, then go W (passing under RR bridge) on Route 8 for about 1.25 mi to gravel road entering from S, then go S on this gravel road .1 mile to campground entrance. The mound is immediately N of the campground road. Signs provide directions to the campground from Route 33. Parking is available adjacent to the mound (Figure 36).

PUBLIC USE: Season and hours: Indian Mound Campground is open from April through November and during the deer hunting season in December. **Fees:** The mound is accessible to campers and non-campers without charge. Fees are charged for camping. **Recreational facilities:** Picnic area, restrooms, hiking, swimming, playground, camping.

EDUCATIONAL FACILITIES: Museum: A small museum is located in the camp store. It features a collection of artifacts found during the excavation of the campground mound, including — among other artifacts — a small number of invertebrate fossils that apparently were collected by the Adena. Some photographs taken during the excavation of the burial mound are also on display. Artifacts from other prehistoric sites, along with natural history specimens, are included in the exhibit.

FOR ADDITIONAL INFORMATION: Contact: Mr. and Mrs. Claire Dunn, (during the camping season) 7896 Roundhouse Road, New Marshfield, OH 45766, 614-664-8700; (during the off-season) 505 Superior Street, Genoa, OH 43430, 419-855-3981.

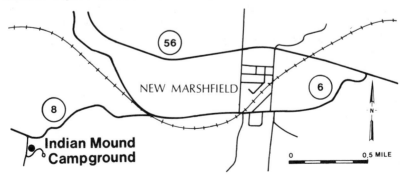

Figure 36. Location of Indian Mound Campground.

63

17. Indian Mound Park

Adena burial mound and (?)Hopewell earthworks
Greene County, Ohio

Two separate features are contained within Indian Mound Park. A flat topped, conical Adena burial mound, the Williamson Mound, is situated on a level upland surface above Massies Creek Gorge. The mound measures 28' high and 156' in circumference at the base; it is reached by a trail that extends about .75 mile through the wooded Massie Creek Gorge. The mound itself lies in an open field not far from the western edge of the gorge. It is mowed on the approach side so that its outline is distinct. Sixty wooden steps lead to the level top.

The Pollock Earthworks, probably Hopewell in origin, are located upon a limestone platform that is nearly isolated from the adjoining land surface by precipitous cliffs descending to the present and former channels of Massies Creek. The works are located about .4 mi southeast of the Williamson Mound. The site consisted originally of four horseshoe-shaped embankments, three small mounds, and a linear embankment broken by three gates (Figure 37). Only the linear embankment is visible today. This site has been under excavation for five years.

The Williamson Mound is reached by a .5 mi foot trail leading NW from the parking lot down the dirt road and across the bridge over Massies Creek, then NE into the forest. The trail is well maintained but not well marked; once in the forest keep to the left to reach the mound. To see the Pollock Earthworks, follow another trail, about .3 mi long, that leads NW from the parking lot.

DIRECTIONS: Follow U. S. Route 42 W from the center of Cedarville about 1 mi to Indian Mound Park on N side of Route 42; an old log cabin is located at the park entrance. Parking is inside the park near the entrance (Figure 38).

PUBLIC USE: Season and hours: The park is open year round during daylight hours. **Fees:** none. **Recreational facilities:** Picnic area, restrooms, hiking (the terrain is beautiful; the Greene County gorges are justifiably well known for their natural beauty), birding.

FOR ADDITIONAL INFORMATION: Contact: Greene County Park District, Xenia, Ohio 45385, 513-376-5140.

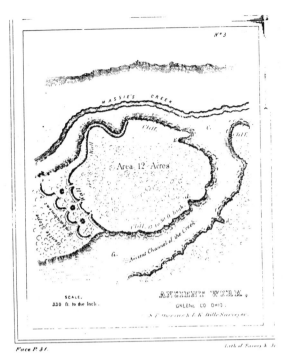

Figure 37. The Pollock Earthworks as depicted in Squier and Davis, 1848.

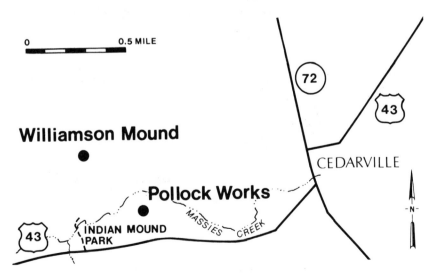

Figure 38. Location of Williamson Mound and Pollock Earthworks in Indian Mound Park.

18. Indian Mounds Park

(?)Adena burial mound
Columbus, Franklin County, Ohio

A single mound is located in the north central part of this public park in south Columbus. Immediately to the north, largely on private property, is another mound. Both mounds lie on a higher terrace of the Scioto River. These mounds probably are Adena burial mounds, but their shape has been altered by farming activities to the extent that they are now low, gently sloping hillocks. In fact, the southeast edge of the park mound forms part of center field for the softball field.

DIRECTIONS: From the intersection of Interstate 270 and U. S. Route 23, go N on Route 23 to Obetz Road (.2 and .7 mi N of I-270 westbound and eastbound exit ramps, respectively), then E .7 mi on Obetz Road, then N 150' on Parsons Avenue to Indian Mounds Park on W side of road (Figure 39).

FOR ADDITIONAL INFORMATION: Contact: Department of Recreation and Parks, City of Columbus, 420 Whittier Street, Columbus, OH 43215, 614-445-3304.

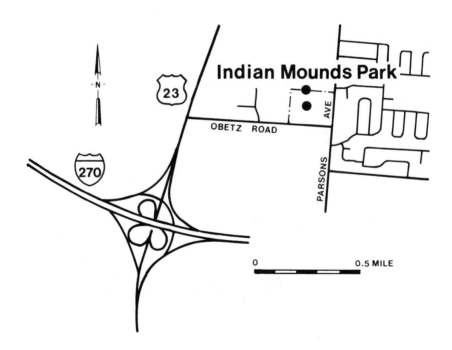

Figure 39. Location of Indian Mounds Park.

19. Marietta Earthworks

Adena, (?)Hopewell, and (?)Mississippian earthworks
Marietta, Washington County, Ohio

In Marietta, Ohio, at the confluence of the Muskingum and Ohio rivers, is an earthworks complex significant for some of its unique features as well as the history of its preservation.

Marietta was established on April 7, 1788, as the first permanent American settlement in the Old Northwest Territory. Founded by the second Ohio Company, Marietta became the capital of the Northwest Territory of the fledgling United States of America. When the first settlers from New England arrived, they found an impressive earthworks complex intact (Figure 40). A large irregular square embankment enclosed over forty acres and contained some (three to five) unusual flat-topped, square mounds — sometimes called truncated pyramids. The largest of these mounds measured 188' × 132' at the base and was about 10' high. From the center of each side of this mound, earthen ramps extend to the ground. A graded way, which the settlers called the *Sacra Via*, led 680' from the square enclosure on the third terrace down to the banks of the Muskingum River. Parallel earthen walls 150' apart lined the *Sacra Via* and rose 20' above its planed surface. Southeast of the large square was a smaller square embankment enclosing about 27 acres, and beyond that was a somewhat truncated conical mound 30' high. The settlers called this mound the *Conus* and believed it to be the grave of an important chieftain. *Conus* was almost completely surrounded by a low circular embankment inside of which was a moat.

In the same year that the town was settled, the Ohio Company passed a resolution to reserve the two enclosures and the mound as commons. Cleared of wild vegetation to form parklands, the earthworks began to erode. In the 1830s the citizens of Marietta established a fund to restore and maintain the mounds and the embankments, an historic preservation effort which is probably the first of its kind west of the Appalachian Mountains.

The most visible element of the Marietta Earthworks today is the large mound, the *Conus*, preserved in Mound Cemetery. It is the prime surviving example of a conical mound with an encircling moat and embankment. The moat measures 15' wide and 4' deep. The base of the embankment is 20' wide and 585' in circumference. Forty five stone steps lead to the top of the *Conus*, where three park benches are located. A time capsule was placed on this mound on July 3, 1976, in commemoration of the U. S. Bicentennial; it is to be opened July 4, 2076. An impressive view of the cemetery is possible from the top of this mound. (Mound Cemetery, opened in 1801, is the burial place for a large number of the early settlers of Marietta, many of

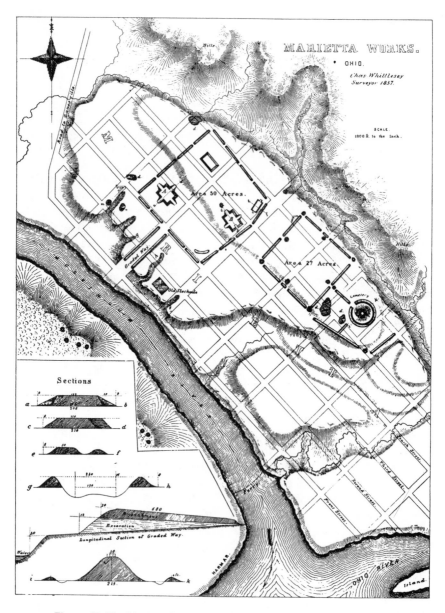

Figure 40. The Marietta Earthworks as depicted in Squier and Davis, 1848.

whom were veterans of the Revolutionary War. It is said that more officers of that war are buried here than in any other single place.)

Two of the square mounds are preserved. The largest, known as the Camp Tupper Earthworks or *Quadranaou*, stands in a park at the head of the graded way between Third Street and Fourth Street. The public library is constructed on top of the second largest elevated square, the *Capitolium* Earthwork, on Fifth Street. The embankments are gone, but the trace of the graded way is preserved as a parkway leading from Third Street to Sacra Via Park on the banks of the Muskingum River. The houses that line the *Sacra Via* today, particularly those on the northwest side, are raised above the graded way's surface, preserving the prehistoric alteration of the second terrace which provided a smooth grade on the pathway from the river up to the earthworks.

DIRECTIONS: Take Exit 1 from Interstate 77 onto State Route 7 (Pike Street), go 2 mi W into the City of Marietta. Just beyond Marietta College, turn NW (right) at traffic lights onto Fourth Street. Go NW 3 blocks to Scammel Street. Turn NE (right) and drive one block E to Mound Cemetery. The main entrance to the cemetery is on Fifth Street at the end of Scammel, but access is possible from Tupper Street also. The other earthworks can be seen by continuing NW on Fifth Street. Between Washington and Warren Streets is the Washington County Public Library, situated on the *Capitolium* Mound. Turn SW (left) at Warren Street and go 1 block to the Camp Tupper Earthworks in the park ahead to your right. At Third Street, Warren Street becomes a divided parkway designated Sacra Via. Continue on Sacra Via to Sacra Via Park at riverside. Curbside parking is available on most of the streets surrounding the remaining earthworks. There is a parking area at Sacra Via Park at the foot of the graded way (Figure 41).

PUBLIC USE: Season and hours: Open daily during daylight hours. **Recreational facilities:** Picnic area in Sacra Via Park. **Restrictions:** Climbing on the *Conus* is prohibited; the offense carries a $50 fine.

FOR ADDITIONAL INFORMATION: Contact: Marietta Tourist and Convention Bureau, 316 Third Street, Marietta, OH 45750, 614-373-5178.

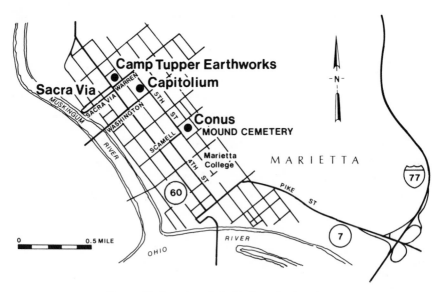

Figure 41. Location of the Marietta Earthworks.

20. Miamisburg Mound State Memorial

Adena burial mound
Miamisburg, Montgomery County, Ohio

The Miamisburg Mound, built on a 100' high bluff east of the Great Miami River, is one of the largest conical burial mounds in eastern North America, being rivaled only by the Grave Creek Mound in Moundsville, West Virginia. Originally the mound was at least 68' high and 877' in circumference at the base. It is now 65' in height, covers about 1.5 acres, and contains an estimated 54,000 cubic yards of earth. The height was lowered as a consequence of a partial excavation undertaken in 1869. At that time a vertical shaft was sunk at least 36' from the top and two horizontal shafts were extended outward from it. Burials were found at the 8' and 36' levels, and various layers of ash, stones and earth were encountered, attesting to the fact that the mound had been used at different time periods and built in increments.

This mound is located in Mound Park. A wooded grassland surrounds the mound, and an excellent view of the City of Miamisburg and the Great Miami River Valley is available from the summit of the mound.

DIRECTIONS: Exit Interstate 75 at Exit 44 (Miamisburg exit), go W on Ohio Route 725 for about 3 miles, then S on South Sixth Street approximately 0.4 mi to Mound Avenue, then S (left) on Mound Avenue about 0.6 mi (passing Mound Golf Course) to S end of Mound Park. The entrance, on your left, is well marked (Figure 42).

PUBLIC USE: Season and Hours: Open year round during daylight hours. **Fees:** None. **Recreational facilities:** Picnic area, playground, restrooms.

FOR ADDITIONAL INFORMATION: Contact: Miamisburg Parks and Recreation Department, 10 N. First Street, Miamisburg. OH 45342, 513-866-3303 *or* Ohio Historical Society, 1985 Velma Ave., Columbus, OH 43211, 614-466-1500.

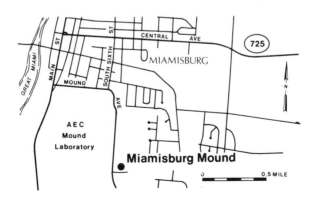

Figure 42. Location of the Miamisburg Mound.

21. Mound Cemetery

Adena burial mound
Meigs County, Ohio

The Mound Cemetery Mound is located in the center of Mound Cemetery. This mound is 11.7' high and 54' in diameter and, based on its location, size, and form, is considered to be an Adena burial mound. Graves of early American settlers in the cemetery date from the 1820s.

DIRECTIONS: Follow Ohio Route 7 N from the village of Chester for 1.5 mi, then NW onto Summer Road for .4 mi. Cemetery is on W side of road (Figure 43).

FOR ADDITIONAL INFORMATION: Contact: Chester Township Trustees, Chester, OH 45720.

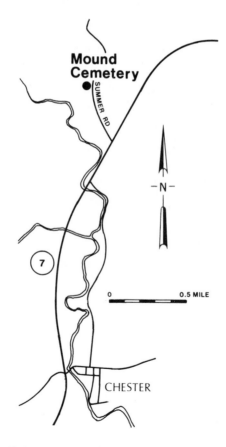

Figure 43. Location of Mound Cemetery (Meigs County).

22. Mound City Group National Monument

Hopewell burial mounds and enclosure
Ross County, Ohio

Mound City is a necropolis, a city of the dead. Within the 13-acre enclosure is one of the greatest concentrations of Hopewell burial mounds known. Squier and Davis considered this the most remarkable of the many Hopewell sites in the Scioto Valley (Figure 44).

Twenty three mounds were contained in the rounded-square enclosure, whose outline resembles that of a typical Hopewell house. The wall of this enclosure is 3'-4' high and 2,050' long. Squier and Davis excavated each of the mounds. Then in 1917 the Army constructed Camp Sherman, a World War I training and detention facility, at Mound City. Twelve mounds were completely leveled, and all of the others except the largest were damaged in some way. Fortunately, the floors of most of the mounds were left intact. After the war, in 1920, William C. Mills of the Ohio State Archaeological and Historical Society directed an excavation of the large remaining mound. Later, after Camp Sherman was dismantled, excavations of the other mound sites continued under the direction of Mills and Henry C. Shetrone and more burials, crematories and caches of grave goods were uncovered. Based on the surveys, descriptions, and excavations of Squier and Davis, Mills, and Shetrone, the Mound City Group has been completely restored. The site was declared a National Monument in 1923.

Generally, each mound within the enclosure covered one or more crematory basins and multiple associated burials. Crematories usually were used repeatedly, sometimes until the floor of the charnel house was filled, or nearly filled, with graves. Then the whole structure was mounded over with earth and capped with stones and gravel. Yet the mounds are not identical in shape, size, or contents, and the more unique grave goods have lent their names to the mounds today. A self guided tour takes the visitor to the Mica Grave, where a cut-away section of the reconstructed mound displays 4 cremated burials, the mode of mound construction and the covering of sheets of mica peculiar to this mound; to the Mound of the Pipes, where Squier and Davis found over 200 effigy pipes (no museum in the United States wanted, or could afford, to buy this collection, so they were sold to a British collector); and to the Death Mask Mound, in which Mills and Shetrone found a headpiece made of human skull bones. In addition, there are the Mound of the Pottery, which contained a beautiful ceremonial vessel decorated with an incised duck motif, and the Mound of the Fossils, in which fragments of mastodon or mammoth tusk were buried. A panoramic view of the entire site is available from the observation balcony above the Visitor Center.

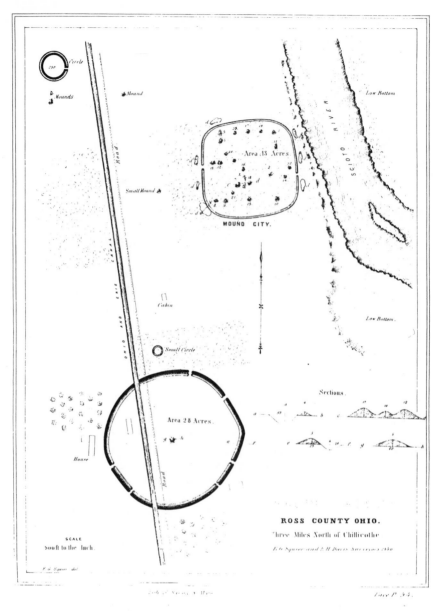

Figure 44. Mound City and environs as depicted in Squier and Davis, 1848.

Directly across the Scioto River from the Mound City Group lies another important Hopewell complex known as the Hopeton Earthworks. These earthworks were mapped by Squier and Davis, but they have never been excavated scientifically. Although they have been damaged by agricultural activities, they are considered to be the best preserved of the complex geometric enclosures of the Hopewell. The earthworks consist of a large circle (diameter = 1,000′) and several small circles attached to a square 950′ × 900′. Parallel embankments extend nearly .5 mile from the main enclosure to a point on the former shoreline of the Scioto River directly opposite Mound City. This orientation of the walls strongly suggests that there was a functional relationship between the two complexes. Both sites probably were used from between about 150 B.C. - A.D. 500. The Hopeton works are privately owned and are not accessible to the public. However, these earthworks might be added to the National Monument in the future.

DIRECTIONS: From U.S. Route 35 at Chillicothe, take Ohio Route 104 N 1.6 mi to the National Monument on the E side of road. Signs along the highways provide directions to Mound City (Figure 45).

PUBLIC USE: Season and Hours: Grounds are open year round during daylight hours. **Fees:** None. **Recreational facilities:** Picnic area, restrooms. **Handicapped facilities:** Most trails, exhibits, and recreational facilities are accessible to the handicapped. **Restrictions:** Climbing on mounds, the use of fires or portable stoves, and camping are prohibited.

EDUCATIONAL FACILITIES: Museum: A large number of artifacts recovered from Mound City are displayed in the Visitor Center as part of an exhibit illustrating the art, fine craftsmanship, trading activities, and burial practices of the Hopewell. Among the artifacts on display are effigy pipes, copper ornaments, mica ornaments, pottery, and obsidian points. An 8-minute videotape interprets Hopewell life and ritual. **Visitor Center hours:** Labor Day to mid-June, 8:00 AM-5:00 PM; Summer hours, 8:00 AM-8:00 PM. The Visitor Center is closed Thanksgiving, Christmas, and New Years Day. **Bookstore:** A small shop in the Visitor Center sells books on archeology and natural history, and other educational materials. **Trails:** A self guided tour leads through the mound and enclosure complex. A .5 mile nature trail is located north of the enclosure; along this trail interpretive signs describe some ways that Indians used the native plants. **Staff programs:** During the summer, ranger-guided activities are provided on weekends and holidays.

FOR ADDITIONAL INFORMATION: Contact: Superintendent, Mound City Group National Monument, 16062 State Route 104, Chillicothe, OH 45601, 614-774-1125. **Read:** Mills, W. C. 1922. "Exploration of the Mound City Group." Ohio Archaeological and Historical Quarterly, vol. 31, pp. 423-584.

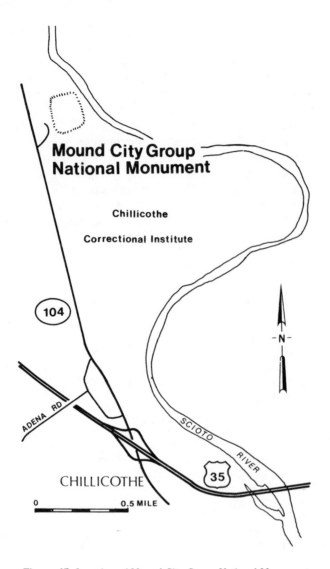

Figure 45. Location of Mound City Group National Monument.

23. Mounds State Park

Adena-Hopewell burial mounds and earthworks
Madison County, Indiana

Mounds State Park contains an unusual array of mounds and enclosures which appear to represent a transition between Adena and Hopewell cultures. On a bench 50'-60' above the White River, 11 features representing two earthworks complexes have been reported within the park. Some of these are well preserved and easily discernible; others are, at best, remarkably subtle. In the southern part of the park is the largest of the earthworks, the Great Mound, a circular enclosure 1,200' in circumference. The embankment averages 6' high and is breached in the south by a single entrance. There is an inner ditch across which a causeway leads to the central platform. A small mound about 45' in diameter was located at the center of the inner platform. One of the park's two unusual fiddle-shaped or panduriform mounds can be seen immediately west of the Great Mound (Figure 46).

About .25 mile upstream in the northern part of the park is the second complex, represented today by a well preserved rectangular enclosure. This also has an interior ditch and raised central platform. Other features, although shown on the Park's trail guide, are difficult or impossible to locate on the grounds.

Excavations in the 1960s uncovered 450 postholes around the perimeter of the central platform of the Great Mound and surrounding the small burial mound on top. This may have been a fence of saplings or small stakes; it had no apparent opening. The small mound had been built in two stages. The primary mound consisted of a platform of three superimposed floors of burned clay. Each floor was covered with a layer of ashes suggesting that the platform had served as the main crematorium for the entire complex. Only one tomb was located within the mound. Constructed of logs, it contained one redeposited cremation and one bundle burial. The log tomb was adjacent to the crematory platform and capped with earth to form the secondary mound. Very few artifacts — some bone awls, some mica, and a platform pipe — were associated with the tomb. (Other burials in the mound were intrusive and probably of Late Woodland origin.) On the basis of pottery and some other resemblances, Great Mound is believed to have been constructed at the same time as a site in Henry County, Indiana, for which radiocarbon dates of A.D. 10 and A.D. 40 have been obtained.

Great Mound presents traits of both the Late Adena and the Hopewell. It may represent a regional variation of Middle Woodland culture restricted to the upper Whitewater and White River drainages.

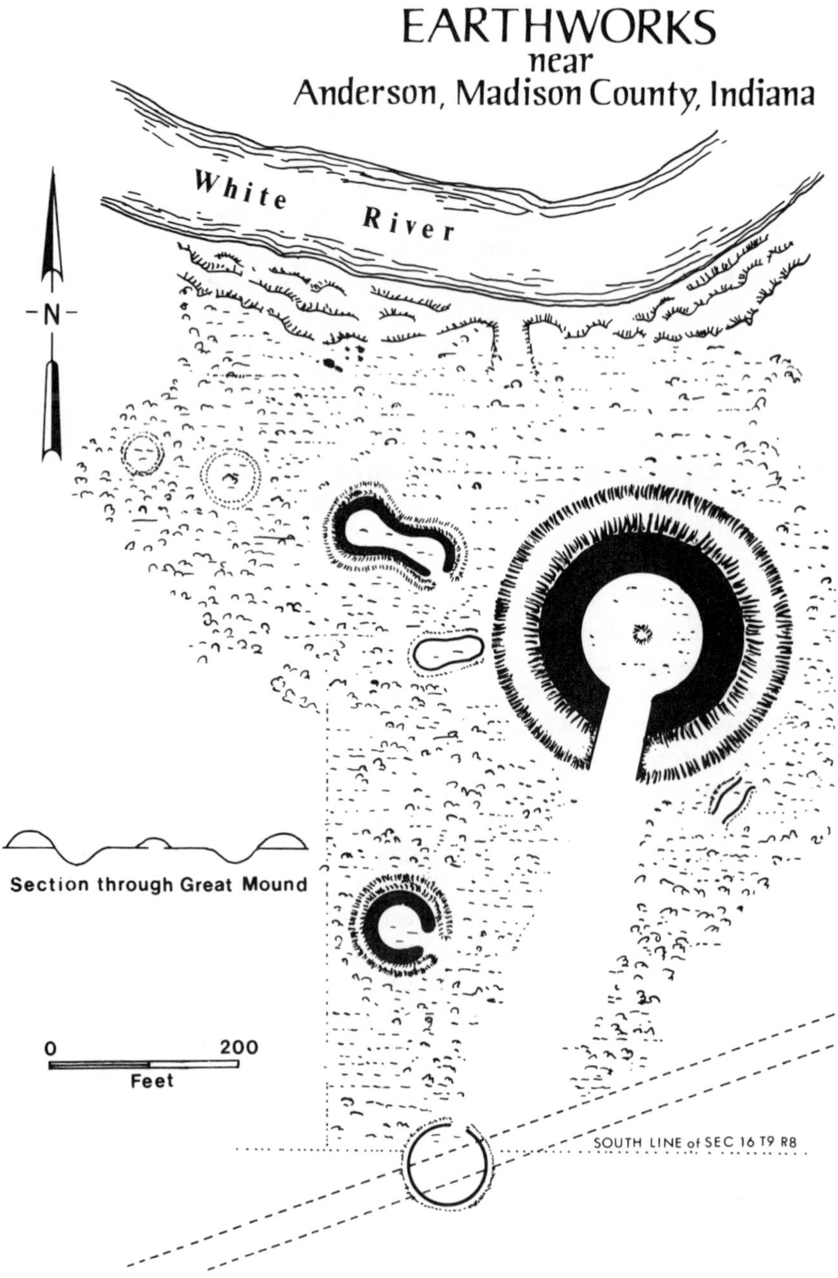

Figure 46. The Anderson Group as depicted in 1937 (after Lilly, 1937).

78

DIRECTIONS: Southbound, exit Interstate 69 at Exit 34, going W on Indiana Route 32 to Indiana Route 232, then W on Route 232 to Mounds State Park (on N side of road). Northbound, exit Interstate 69 at Exit 26 going N on Indiana Route 9 to Route 232, then E on Route 232 to Mounds State Park (Figure 47).

PUBLIC USE: Season and Hours: The park is open year round. **Fees:** From mid-April through Labor Day, admission is $1.50 per car per day; From Labor Day through October, admission is $1.50 per day only on weekends; From November 1 to mid-April, there is no admission fee. **Recreational facilities:** Picnic area, restrooms, camping, horseback riding, fishing, hiking, cross-country skiing, and water sports.

EDUCATIONAL FACILITIES: Museum: A nature center is located in the Bronnenberg House just south of the park entrance. This center contains an exhibit on the park's mounds, including a scale model of the park showing the location of the mounds and a model of an Adena house. **Nature Center hours:** 8:00 AM-4:30 PM, daily from mid-April through Labor Day. **Trails:** Great Mound and other earthworks in the southern part of the park are reached by a short walk along either Trail #1 or the bridle path. These trails are scenic, well maintained, and traverse relatively level terrain.

FOR ADDITIONAL INFORMATION: Contact: Superintendent, Mounds State Park, Anderson, IN 46013, 317-642-6627. **Read:** (1) Vickery, Kent D. 1970. Preliminary report on the excavation of the "Great Mound" at Mounds State Park in Madison County, Indiana. Proceedings of the Indiana Academy of Science for 1969, vol. 79, pp. 75-82. (2) Swartz, B. K., Jr. 1976. "Mounds State Park." Central States Archaeological Journal, vol. 23, pp. 26-32.

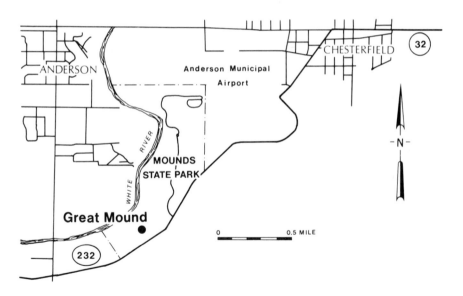

Figure 47. Location of Mounds State Park.

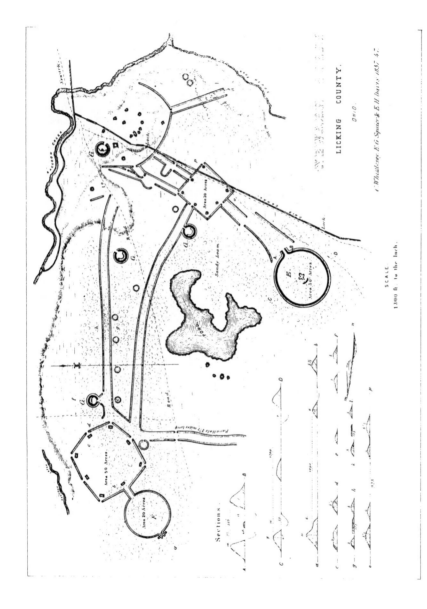

Figure 48. The Newark Earthworks as depicted in Squier and Davis, 1848.

24. Newark Earthworks

Hopewell mounds and geometric enclosures
Newark, Licking County, Ohio

The Newark Earthworks were one of the most extensive and diverse complexes of prehistoric earthworks in the eastern United States (Figure 48). An array of circles, squares, octagons, parallel embankments and circular and elliptical mounds covered about 4 square miles. Most of these features were located on the second terrace above the three tributaries of the Licking River which converge at Newark. This site, like so many other Hopewell earthworks complexes, lies near the boundary separating the relatively level glaciated Central Lowland and the hilly unglaciated Appalachian Plateau regions of Ohio. In addition, the Newark Earthworks are near Flint Ridge, and villages at or near the earthworks may have benefitted from this relative location as important inter-regional trading centers. Most of the Newark Earthworks have been destroyed by agriculture, transportation developments, and urban growth; but four parts of the complex, including most of its two largest units, remain.

One of the two remaining large features is incorporated in Moundbuilders State Memorial. This partly wooded tract of 66 acres includes a large circular earthworks enclosing 26 acres and measuring about 1,200' in diameter with walls 8'-14' high. A ditch encircles the interior base of the wall. An opening in the circular wall faces east-northeast. A cluster of four small mounds (or perhaps a bird-like effigy mound) and an arcuate mound are located in the center of the circle. Two parallel walls extend northeastward from either side of the opening in the Great Circle to the edge of the Memorial grounds. The Great Circle became the site of the Licking County Fairgrounds around 1853 and served in that capacity well into the 20th Century. A track for horse racing was located inside the circle. Between 1892 and 1908, this area was used as a campground by the National Guard. Consequently some of the features were altered or destroyed, but have since been restored by the Ohio Historical Society.

A second large tract, the 120 acre Octagon State Memorial, encompasses an interconnected large octagon and circle earthworks and a small circular feature located just beyond the southeastern edge of the octagon. The octagon, enclosing 50 acres, was the largest single feature in the Newark complex, whereas the circle connected to it encompasses 20 acres. Octagon, too, was a part of the National Guard encampment until 1908, at which time control reverted to the City of Newark and a golf course was built. Today the Memorial is owned by the Ohio Historical Society and leased to the Mound Builders Country Club, which maintains the grounds as a private golf course (Figure 15).

Wright Earthworks State Memorial consists of a corner of what was once a large square enclosure of 20 acres.

A small, low conical mound — the Owen Mound — about 6' high, is located on the grounds of the Newark High School's Evans Athletic Complex, near the end of the parking lot and the entrance to the building.

DIRECTIONS: All of the sites are located in the western part of Newark (Figure 49). (1) The entrance to Moundbuilders State Memorial is from Ohio Route 79. (2) The Wright Earthworks is reached by taking 21st Street to Burt Avenue, then E on Burt Avenue to Williams Street, then N on Williams Street to Waldo Street, then E on Waldo Street to James Street. The Memorial lies on the E side of James Street, directly across from the end of Waldo Street. (3) Octagon State Memorial is reached via 30th Street either from Route 79 or Route 16 (via Church Street). Follow 30th Street to Parkview, then W on Parkview (one-way) to Memorial grounds. Parking is ahead and to right at end of Parkview. (4) Owen Mound is reached by following Sharon Valley Road W from Granville Street for 1 mi to the Evans Athletic Complex on N side of road. Enter Evans Athletic Complex, follow driveway to the end; the mound is visible from the driveway.

PUBLIC USE: Season and Hours: Moundbuilders State Memorial grounds are open 9:30 AM-5:00 PM, Wednesday through Saturday, Noon-5:00 PM, Sunday and holidays, Memorial Day through Labor Day; Same hours, weekends only, Labor Day through October. The grounds are closed November through Memorial Day. The other sites are open year round during daylight hours. **Fees:** None. **Recreational facilities:** (available only at Moundbuilders State Memorial; enter from corner of 21st and Cooper streets) Picnic area, restrooms. **Restrictions:** Octagon State Memorial is privately managed as a private golf course. Mound Builders Country Club requests that visitors please check with the groundskeeper in the grey building just inside the octagon wall before venturing onto the golf course.

EDUCATIONAL FACILITIES: Museum: The first museum in the United States devoted exclusively to the art of prehistoric American Indians was opened at Moundbuilders State Memorial in 1971. Today, this museum contains exhibits of Indian art in copper, stone and ceramic media, along with artifacts from the Archaic through the Mississippian periods. A life-sized diorama depicts Indians working with a cache of Flint Ridge flint. Outside, near the museum entrance, is a bronze scale model relief map based on the survey of the Newark Earthworks published by Squier and Davis. It shows how the earthworks appeared in 1847. The surviving portions are burnished. **Museum hours:** Same as grounds hours (above). **Fees:** Admission $1.50 adults, $1.00 children 6-12. **Bookstore:** The museum has a small selection of books on archeology and natural history, and other educational materials. **Trails:** A footpath leads from the museum and picnic areas at Moundbuilders State Memorial to and around the Great Circle Earthworks.

FOR ADDITIONAL INFORMATION: Contact: Ohio Historical Society, 1985 Velma Avenue, Columbus, OH 43211, 614-466-1500; Newark Area Chamber of Commerce, 50 W Locust Street, Newark, OH 43055, 614-345-9757; *or* Newark Board of Education, E Main and 1st streets, Newark, OH 43055, 614-345-9891. **Read:** Hooge, P., and others. n.d. "Discovering the prehistoric mound builders of Licking County, Ohio." Newark: The Licking County Archaeological and Landmarks Society.

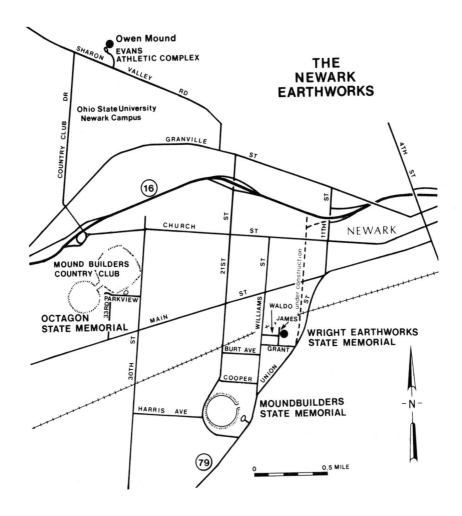

Figure 49. Location of the Newark Earthworks.

25. Norwood Mound

(?)Adena burial mound
Norwood, Hamilton County, Ohio

This elliptical mound measuring 13.5' high and 130' × 100' in basal diameters is located on a high hill above downtown Norwood. The mound has not been excavated, but its size, shape and upland location suggest that it is an Adena burial mound.

DIRECTIONS: Follow Montgomery Road (combined U. S. Route 22 and Ohio Route 3) N from downtown Norwood .5 mi, then SE on Indian Mound Avenue .25 mi to Norwood Mound. The mound is reached by a lane that leads S several yards from Indian Mound Avenue (Figure 50).

FOR ADDITIONAL INFORMATION: Contact: City of Norwood, Norwood, OH 45212, 513-396-8200.

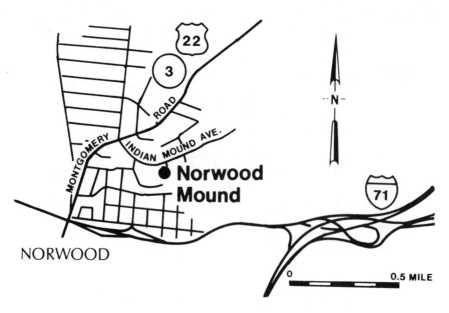

Figure 50. Location of Norwood Mound.

26. Orator's Mound

Adena burial mound
Greene County, Ohio

Orator's Mound, so named because a pavillion from which speeches were given once crowned its summit, is a small (5' high; 45' × 39' at the base) mound located on high ground midway between two branches of Yellow Springs Creek, 1.4 miles north of its confluence with the Little Miami River. Yellow Springs, a perpetually flowing mineral spring, rises 550' northwest of the mound. Part of Orator's Mound has been excavated, and evidence recovered indicates that it represents the Late Adena period. Orator's Mound, also known as Glen Helen Mound, lies about 20' south of the Inman Nature Trail in Glen Helen.

DIRECTIONS: From U. S. Route 68 in Yellow Springs, follow Ohio Route 343 E about 750', then S on Old Stage Road 500', then continue S about 1,000' beyond where Old Stage Road departs to SE. Alternate route is to follow Corry Street S from U. S. Route 68 .45 mi to Trailside Museum on E side of road, then take foot trail about .3 mi to mound. Parking is available at both locations (Figure 51).

EDUCATIONAL FACILITIES: Museum: Trailside Museum has exhibits interpreting the natural and cultural history of the Glen Helen region. **Bookstore:** The museum gift shop sells books on history and natural history, along with other educational materials. **Trails:** An intricate system of trails leads through all parts of Glen Helen. The Inman Trail, a scenic self guiding nature trail about 1 mi in length, leads past the Orator's Mound and other significant features of the Glen.

FOR ADDITIONAL INFORMATION: Contact: Glen Helen, Antioch University, 405 Corry Street, Yellow Springs, OH 45387, 513-767-7375.

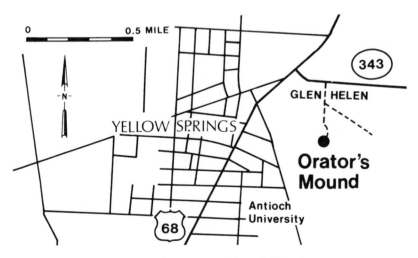

Figure 51. Location of Orator's Mound.

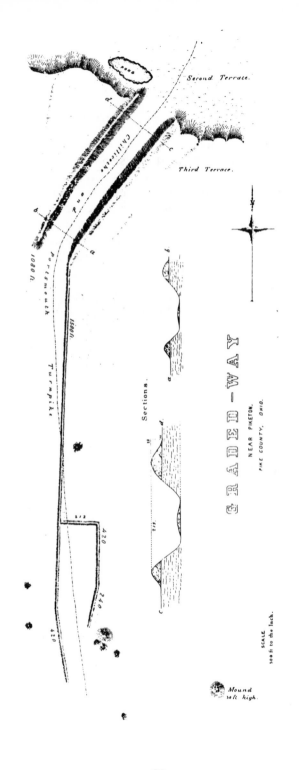

Figure 52. The Piketon Earthworks as depicted in Squier and Davis, 1848. The cluster of four mounds near the left edge of the illustration are >rved in Piketon's Mound Cemetery. Notice the graded way north of the cemetery mounds.

86

27. Piketon Mound Cemetery

(?)Adena burial mounds
Pike County, Ohio

The four mounds in Mound Cemetery at Piketon exemplify the more ordinary mounds which dotted the Scioto Valley at the time of Anglo-American settlement. Squier and Davis, writing in 1848, said:

> "It is common to find two or three, sometimes four or five, sepulchre mounds in a group. In such cases it is always to be remarked that one of the group is much the largest, twice or three times the dimensions of any of the others; and that the smaller ones, of various sizes, are arranged around its base, generally joining it, thus evincing a designed dependence and intimate relation between them."

The largest of the Piketon mounds is about 25' high; the 3 smaller mounds vary between 5' and 10' in height. In one of the small mounds the skeleton of a girl wrapped in bark was found.

This mound group lay near one of the most magnificent of known graded ways (Figure 52). The way passed in a generally north-south direction from the third terrace to the second terrace of the Scioto River, now 17' below. The way was 1,080' long and over 200' wide. (In the 19th Century the Chillicothe and Portsmouth turnpike passed through the bordering embankments.) At places the dirt thrown up to level the passage formed an embankment 22' above the graded surface. The eastern wall, now obliterated by cultivation, extended southward another 2,580' toward the cemetery mounds. Most of this impressive earthwork has been destroyed by modern highway construction and the extraction of underlying gravel.

DIRECTIONS: Follow U.S. Route 23 S from Piketon, exit onto Ohio Route 124, go E .4 mi, crossing Beaver Creek, then N at tavern for .4 mi to Mound Cemetery on E side of road (Figure 53).

PUBLIC USE: Season and hours: Open year round during daylight hours.

FOR ADDITIONAL INFORMATION: Contact: Town of Piketon, Piketon, OH 45661, 614-289-2581.

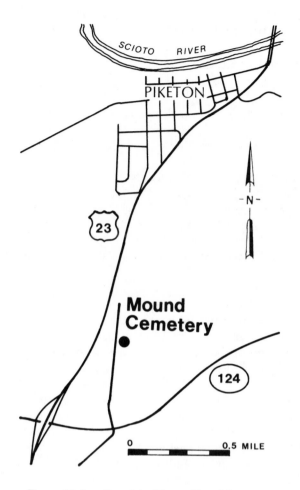

Figure 53. Location of the Piketon Mound Cemetery.

28. Portsmouth Mound Park

Hopewell earthworks
Portsmouth, Scioto County, Ohio

At the confluence of the Scioto and Ohio Rivers, the Hopewell constructed their most elongate single system of earthworks. From the vicinity of Mound Park in Portsmouth, parallel walls radiated toward the Ohio River and were continued on the Kentucky side of the river, where they led to two geometric enclosures. Extending 8 miles along the Ohio, the embankments represented 20 miles of earthwork construction (Figure 54). The one horseshoe-shaped platform near the southwestern corner of Mound Park, Horseshoe Mound, is all that remains of this impressive complex in Ohio. It was one of a pair of horseshoe-shaped raised platforms that lay at the heart of this earthwork system. Both platforms measured 80' × 70'. Part of the square works in Kentucky is preserved on private land in South Portsmouth. The rest has been destroyed by agricultural and urban development in the 19th and 20th centuries.

DIRECTIONS: From U.S. Route 23 go E on Kinneys Lane approximately .75 mi (to three blocks past Greenlawn Cemetery), then S on Hutchins Avenue for .3 mi (2 blocks) to Mound Park. From U.S. 52 go N on Hutchins Avenue .25 mi (3 blocks) to Mound Park. Curbside parking is available at the park (Figure 55).

PUBLIC USE: Season and hours: Open daily. **Fees:** None. **Recreation facilities:** Picnic area, restrooms, game fields. **Restrictions:** Walking on or in the earthworks is prohibited. Dogs are not allowed in the park.

FOR ADDITIONAL INFORMATION: Contact: City of Portsmouth, Portsmouth, OH 45662, 614-354-8807 *or* Portsmouth Area Chamber of Commerce, P. O. Box 509, Portsmouth, OH 45662, 614-353-1116.

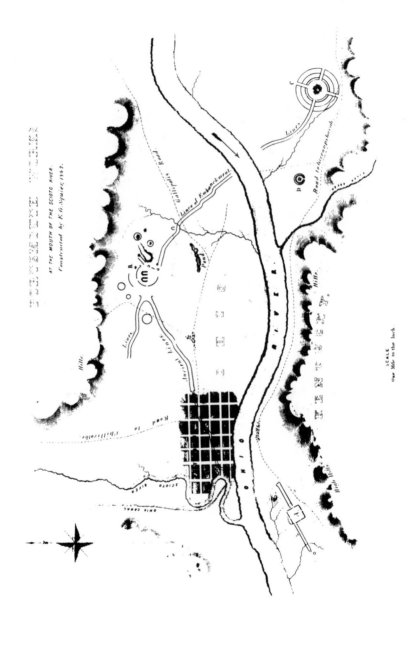

Figure 54. The Portsmouth Earthworks as depicted in Squier and Davis, 1848. As is true for Hopewell earthworks complexes generally, most of this extensive system has been destroyed. Only the eastern "horseshoe" remains in public ownership.

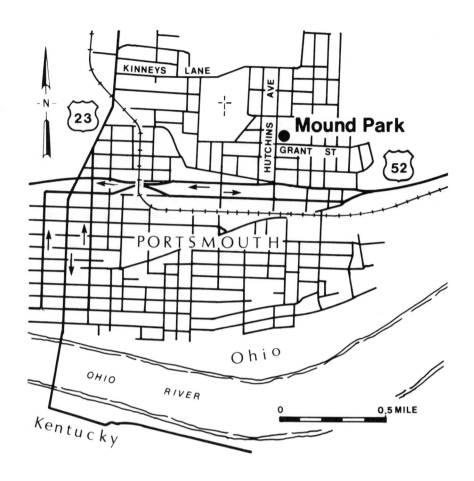

Figure 55. Location of Portsmouth Mound Park.

29. Reynolds Mound

(?)Adena burial mound
Pleasants County, West Virginia

This feature is approximately 16' high and is probably an Adena burial mound. This mound is located immediately southeast of West Virginia Route 2; it is mowed, readily visible, and stands as sentinel at the entrance to a residential area.

DIRECTIONS: Follow West Virginia Route 2 NE from the St. Marys-Newport Bridge for 2.9 mi. The mound is on SE side of road. A residential street, Mound Manor, loops around the mound (Figure 56).

FOR ADDITIONAL INFORMATION: Contact: Blennerhassett Historical Park Commission, Parkersburg, WV 26101.

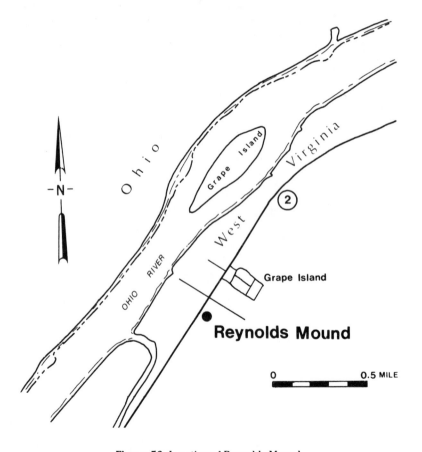

Figure 56. Location of Reynolds Mound.

30. Seip Mound State Memorial

Hopewell burial mounds and earthworks
Ross County, Ohio

Seip Mound State Memorial preserves less than one tenth of a major Hopewell ceremonial center. The rest of the earthworks and mounds are on private land and have been nearly obliterated through long agricultural use.

Situated on the second and third terraces north of Paint Creek, Seip (pronounced sipe) consisted of a square and a complete circle joined by a larger irregular circle and enclosed a total of 121 acres (Figure 57). The walls were 10′ high, 50′ wide at the base, and 10,000′ long. Within the embankment were several small mounds, 3 large conjoined mounds and the exceptionally large oblong central mound that now dominates the 10 acre Memorial. Large mounds like Seip, which originally measured 250′ × 150′ × 30′, are unusual in Hopewell sites; only the central mound (500′ × 180′ × 33′) of the Hopewell Group itself was larger than the one at Seip.

The large mound was excavated in 1925-26 by Henry C. Shetrone and Emerson Greenman of the Ohio State Archaeological and Historical Society

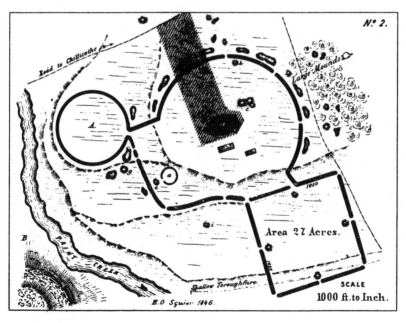

Figure 57. Seip Earthworks as depicted in Squier and Davis, 1848. The lightly shaded portion is preserved as Seip State Memorial.

and then restored to its present form. They reported 122 burials, both cremations and extended burials. Grave goods included mica from the Carolinas, copper from Isle Royale in Lake Superior, and effigy pipes from the Tennessee River Valley. Most notable perhaps were some 15,000 freshwater pearls of various sizes and shapes. The value of these pearls, when new, was estimated in 1960 to have been equivalent to about $2,000,000!

Much of our knowledge of Hopewell life comes from recent excavations of the Seip complex. In the 1970s the postmold patterns of 10 Hopewell structures were unearthed; the outlines of three may be seen in front of the mound. All had two opposing walls of double post construction and two of single posts. Hopewell houses were square or rectangular. Occupational debris and the lack of hearths or fire pits suggest that these buildings were the workshops of the highly skilled artisans who produced the funerary objects for which the Hopewell are famous. The people who built the embankments, crafted the ceremonial objects, and prepared the dead lived outside the enclosure, where at least one large village site has been located.

Seip Mound State Memorial is jointly managed as an historical site and a roadside rest area on the south side of U.S. Route 50 between Chillicothe and Hillsboro.

DIRECTIONS: Follow U. S. Route 50 approximately 17 mi W of Chillicothe, 4 mi W of Bourneville, 3 mi E of Bainbridge, or 22 mi E of Hillsboro. Signs identifying the roadside rest appear about 1 mi on either side of the site (Figure 58).

PUBLIC USE: Season and hours: Open year round, 6:00 AM-9:00 PM. **Fees:** None. **Recreational facilities:** Picnic area, restrooms. **Restrictions:** Pets must be leashed and are allowed only in designated exercise areas.

EDUCATIONAL FACILITIES: Interpretative center: Exhibits in an outdoor pavilion provide an overview of the archeology of Ohio and more detailed information on the Seip complex and the history of its exploration. Some artifacts recovered from Seip are on display. The floor plans of the houses or workshops have been reconstructed on site, at scale, inside the earthwork. **Trail:** A dirt trail leads through the earthwork, past the workshop sites, to the top of the central mound.

FOR ADDITIONAL INFORMATION: Contact: Ohio Historical Society, 1985 Velma Avenue, Columbus, OH 43211, 614-466-1500. **Read:** (1) Mills, W.C. 1909. "Explorations of the Seip Mound." Ohio Archaeological and Historical Quarterly, vol. 18, pp. 269-321. (2) Shetrone, H. C. and E. F. Greenman. 1931. "Explorations of the Seip Group of prehistoric earthworks." Ohio Archaeological and Historical Quarterly, vol. 40, pp. 343-509. (3) Baby, R. S., and S. M. Langlois. 1979. "Seip Mound State Memorial: Nonmortuary aspects of Hopewell." Pp. 18-18 *in* D. S. Brose and N. Greber (eds.), Hopewell archaeology. Kent, Ohio: Kent State University Press. (4) Greber, N. 1979. "A comparative study of site morphology and burial patterns at Edwin Harness Mound and Seip mounds 1 and 2." Pp. 27-38 *in* D. S. Brose and N. Greber (eds.), Hopewell archaeology. Kent, Ohio: Kent State University Press.

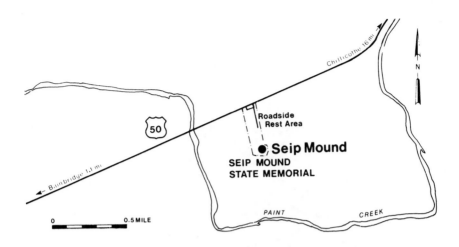

Figure 58. Location of Seip Mound and Earthworks.

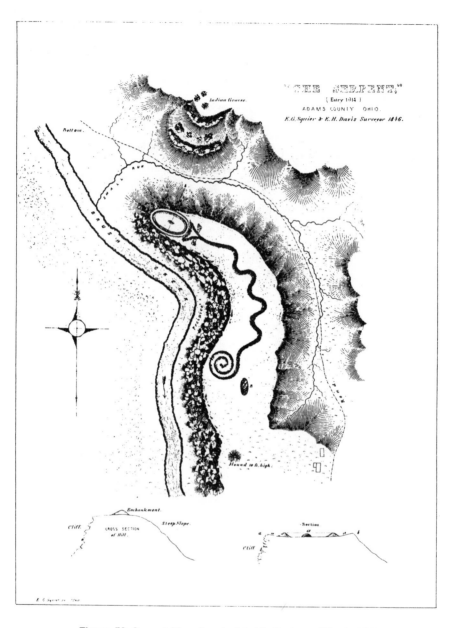

Figure 59. Serpent Mound as depicted in Squier and Davis, 1848.

96

31. Serpent Mound State Memorial

(?)Adena effigy mound
Adams County, Ohio

Serpent Mound, largest of the effigy mounds, is perhaps the best known example of the mound builders' work in the middle Ohio Valley. Writhing across a ridgetop, the total length of the Serpent is 1,348' — approximately .25 mile (Figure 59). The core of the base is made of clay and rocks; these were covered with soil to a height of 4'-5'. The average width of the body is 20'. The Serpent lies more than 100' above Ohio Brush Creek on the very eastern margin of the Interior Low Plateaus province. The immediate area is of geologic importance, for the Serpent was constructed on an unusual cryptoexplosion structure. Nearly circular in map view and with a diameter of 4.5-5 miles, the cryptoexplosion structure is extensively faulted as a result of two gas explosions that occurred beneath the surface in the geologic past.

At one time this effigy mound was considered to be a mark of God that indicated the location of the Garden of Eden. Today, however, it is generally agreed that the mound was constructed by Adena people, although the evidence for this lies not in the effigy itself but in several nearby conical burial mounds.

There have been various interpretations of the shape of the head of the Serpent. Some views held that it was carrying an egg or that it was about to catch a frog, for example. The most prevalent modern opinion is that it represents the open mouth of a striking snake as seen from above. Visitors to Serpent State Memorial can have a bird's-eye view of the effigy from atop an observation tower.

Serpent Mound was excavated by Fredric Ward Putnam, the "Father of American Archaeology". The mound became especially well known after Putnam's collections from the site were exhibited at the Chicago World Fair in 1893. Less well known is Putnam's successful campaign to preserve the Serpent. When the mound was about to be sold and thus faced almost certain destruction, Putnam managed to raise $5,880 by private subscription in Boston. The mound was purchased with this money in 1887 and given in trust to Harvard University's Peabody Museum, where Putnam was Curator of Archaeology and Ethnology. In recognition of Putnam's efforts at preservation, the Ohio legislature, in 1888, passed the nation's first law for the protection of archeological sites. Nationwide interest in the coiling snake effigy was to lead to programs across the country for the preservation of archeological sites as state or national parks. In 1900 Harvard deeded the effigy to the State of Ohio, stipulating that it be preserved and always be open to the public. It became one of Ohio's first State Memorials.

DIRECTIONS: From Locust Grove follow Ohio Route 73 N 4 mi to park entrance on N side of highway. From Hillsboro, follow Ohio Route 73 S 18 mi to park entrance (Figure 60).

PUBLIC USE: Season and Hours: 9:30 AM-5:00 PM, Wednesday through Saturday, Noon-5:00 PM, Sunday and holidays, Memorial Day through Labor Day; same hours, weekends only, Labor Day through October. Closed November through Memorial Day. **Fees:** Admission $2.00 per car. **Food service:** Snack bar. **Recreational facilities:** Picnic area, restrooms. **Restrictions:** Climbing on mounds is not permitted. Pets must be on leash.

EDUCATIONAL FACILITIES: Museum: The museum contains exhibits on the archeology of Serpent Mound as well as the unique geology of the area. A diorama of the construction of the Serpent and a model of an Adena burial mound are prominent among the exhibits. Some of the artifacts excavated by Putnam are on display. **Museum hours:** Same as grounds hours (above). **Fees:** Park entry fee includes admission to museum. **Bookstore:** A small selection of books on archeology and natural history, and other educational materials, are sold in the museum gift shop. **Trail:** A paved path leads to and around the Serpent.

FOR ADDITIONAL INFORMATION: Contact: Ohio Historical Society, 1985 Velma Avenue, Columbus, OH 43211, 614-466-1500.

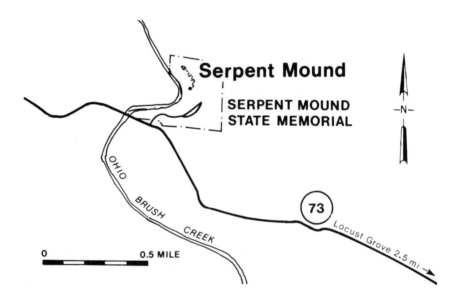

Figure 60. Location of Serpent Mound.

32. Shawnee Lookout Park

Burial mounds and Hopewell hilltop enclosure
Hamilton County, Ohio

The 975 acre Shawnee Lookout Park contains a rich and diverse array of burial mounds, earthworks, habitation sites, and other archeological features documenting more than 10,000 years of Indian occupation of the region. The most significant earthwork in this park is Miami Fort, which occupies the relatively level summit of an elevated peninsula of land wedged between the Ohio and Great Miami rivers at their confluence (Figure 61). Lying 300' above the rivers, the fort walls, built on the side of the hill near its crest, varied from 1'-12' in height and enclosed an area of about 12 acres. The wall was built, at least in part, of earth from within the enclosure laid upon a fire-hardened clay base and reinforced along the outer edge with low stone retaining walls. Wood also might have been used to build the walls. Several breaks or "gateways" separated segments of the walls. A radiocarbon dated sample of burned earth suggests that construction of the fort began around A.D. 270. Evidence of habitation within the enclosure suggests that some of the builders of the fort actually lived within its walls, at least for a short time.

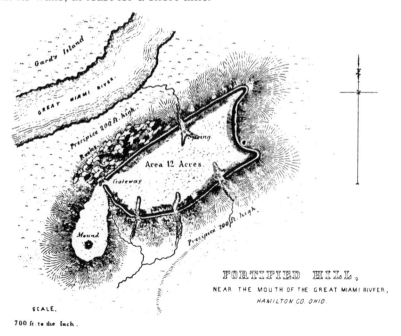

Figure 61. Miami Fort as depicted in Squier and Davis, 1848.

99

Among the other mounds known from within the park are three confirmed or suspected burial mounds occupying a promontory immediately southwest of the fort. The largest measures 6' high and 90' in diameter. A partial excavation of this mound in 1966 yielded remains of at least 6 human skeletons. An adjacent village site, also excavated in 1966, apparently was occupied during both Early Adena (800 B.C.-300 B.C.) and Late Adena-Hopewell, or Middle Woodland, (A.D. 1-A.D. 700) periods. This information indicates that the upland surface was inhabited before Miami Fort was built, and allows that the fort could have been built during the second, or Middle Woodland, occupation.

Other mounds and village sites within the park are described in the Miami Fort Trail Guide and in the park museum.

DIRECTIONS: At Lawrenceburg, Indiana, exit Interstate 275, go E on U.S. Route 50 about 6 mi, then W on Mt. Nebo Road about 500', then W on Miamiview Road about 4 mi to park. Signs provide direction to park. Parking is available in park (Figure 62).

PUBLIC USE: Season and hours: Open year round during daylight hours. **Fees:** $1.00 per day, $3.00 per year for motor vehicles. **Recreational facilities:** Picnic area, restrooms, hiking, golf course, boat launch.

EDUCATIONAL FACILITIES: Museum: The Shawnee Lookout Archaeological Museum contains exhibits depicting the archeology of Shawnee Lookout Park and environs. Most of the artifacts on display were excavated from Shawnee Lookout Park. **Museum hours:** 1:00 PM-5:00 PM, weekends and holidays, Memorial Day through Labor Day. **Trails:** The Miami Fort Trail, 1.4 miles in length, leads from a parking lot at the base of the fort hill through Miami Fort to the west end of the elevated promontory. Nine recorded archeological sites, including the fort itself, are located along the trail. Be certain to obtain a copy of the well-written Miami Fort Trail Guide to take on the trail.

FOR ADDITIONAL INFORMATION: Contact: Hamilton County Park District, 10245 Winton Road, Cincinnati, OH 45231, 513-521-7275. **Read:** Starr, S. F. 1960. "The Archaeology of Hamilton County, Ohio." Journal of the Cincinnati Museum of Natural History, vol. 23, no. 1.

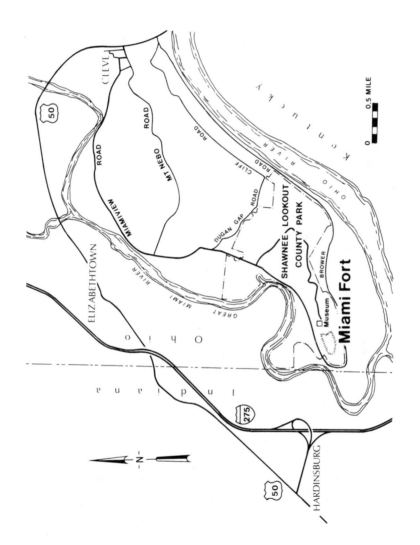

Figure 62. Location of Shawnee Lookout Park.

101

33. Shawnee Reservation Mound

Adena burial mound
Institute, Kanawha County, West Virginia

The Shawnee Reservation Mound, also known as the Institute Fairgrounds Mound and the Poorhouse Mound, is located in Shawnee Regional Park and lies immediately west of the clubhouse. This mound is presently about 20' high and 80' in basal diameter, but was originally 25' high and greater than 80' in diameter. The Bureau of Ethnology partially excavated this mound during the 1880s, at which time at least three burials or cremations were found. The mound is attributed to the late Adena period. This is one of only three mounds that remain of the once extensive Adena mound and earthworks complex (which contained about 50 mounds and 10 earthworks) that centered upon the Charleston area of the Kanawha Valley. The others are the South Charleston, or Criel, Mound and a privately owned mound.

DIRECTIONS: Exit Interstate 64 in Institute, West Virginia, onto West Virginia Route 25, go E about .8 mi on Route 25 to Shawnee Regional Park on S side of highway. Mound is about 800' SW of Route 25. Parking is available at park (Figure 63).

FOR ADDITIONAL INFORMATION: Contact: General Manager, Shawnee Regional Park, P. O. Box 267, Institute, West Virginia 25112, 304-768-7600.

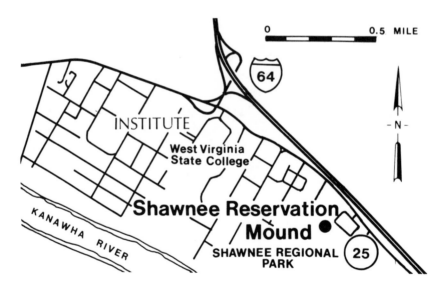

Figure 63. Location of Shawnee Reservation Mound.

34. Shorts Woods Park Mound

Adena burial mound
Cincinnati, Hamilton County, Ohio

The Shorts Woods Park Mound is located in the eastern part of Shorts Woods Golf Course. The elliptical mound is 8.3' high and 113' × 90' in basal diameters. The mound is fenced, but can be viewed from near the intersection of Fernbank and Dahlia Avenues or the northwest end of Home City Avenue.

DIRECTIONS: Follow U. S. Route 50 W from downtown Cincinnati about 9 mi to Lee Park, then N on Elco Street .25 mi, then NW on Home City Avenue .4 mi to Shorts Woods Golf Course. The mound lies near the end of Home City Avenue (Figure 64).

FOR ADDITIONAL INFORMATION: Contact: Cincinnati Park Board, 950 Eden Park Drive, Cincinnati, OH 45202, 513-352-4080.

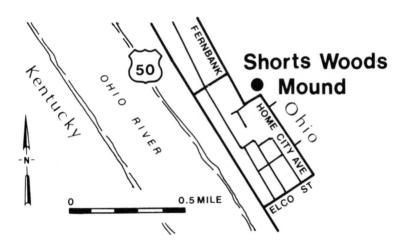

Figure 64. Location of Shorts Woods Park Mound.

35. South Charleston Mound

Adena burial mound
South Charleston, Kanawha County, West Virginia

Extending for 8 miles along the upper terraces of the Kanawha River floodplain, in the vicinity of modern Charleston, West Virginia, was the second largest concentration of Adena mounds and circular enclosures known. In 1894, Cyrus Thomas reported 50 mounds ranging from 3' to 35' in height and from 35' to 200' in diameter, and 8 to 10 circular earthworks enclosing from 1 to 30 acres, in this area. Stone mounds dotted the bluffs above the floodplain.

The South Charleston, or Criel, Mound is the second largest of the burial mounds and one of the very few mounds that remain of this once important group. (One small mound has survived in a private cemetery in South Charleston, while another — the Shawnee Reservation Mound — still exists in Institute.) Criel Mound is the centerpiece of a small municipal park in South Charleston. The conical mound was originally 33' high and 520' in diameter. It lay equidistant between two "sacred circles" each 556' in diameter. The top of Criel Mound was leveled during the 19th Century for the erection of a judge's stand associated with a racetrack which circled its base. The South Charleston Mound is the second largest mound surviving in West Virginia; Grave Creek Mound in Moundsville is the largest.

In 1883-84 an excavation under the auspices of the Bureau of Ethnology uncovered 13 burials at two different levels in the mound. Most interesting were the 11 skeletons lying on a layer of bark near the base of the mound. One body with a copper headdress lay in the middle. The others bodies were arranged 5 on each side in a semicircle with the feet directed toward the central skeleton. Each of the eastern 5 bodies had been buried with an unused lance head. Next to the northernmost one were a fish dart, three arrowheads, and some mussel shells. Nothing was found with the western 5 bodies. All 11 skeletons were apparently buried in a wooden structure about 16' in diameter and with a conical roof.

DIRECTIONS: Exit Interstate 64 onto Montrose Street, go N about .15 mi to end of Montrose, then W on U. S. Route 60 (MacCorkle Avenue) .5 mi to Seventh Avenue, then SW onto Seventh Avenue .1 mi to South Charleston Mound, on N side of street. Metered parking is available at the park on D Street and Seventh Avenue (Figure 65).

FOR ADDITIONAL INFORMATION: Contact: South Charleston Chamber of Commerce, 607 D Street, South Charleston, WV 25303, 304-744-0051.

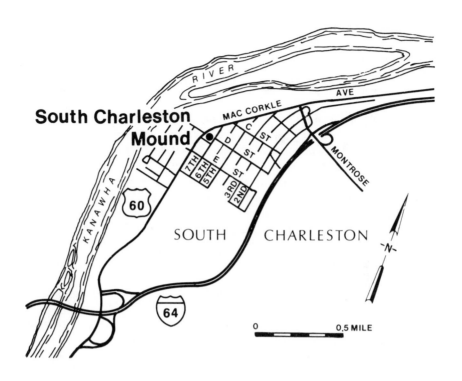

Figure 65. Location of South Charleston Mound.

36. Story Mound

Adena burial mound
Chillicothe, Ross County, Ohio

Story Mound is a conical burial mound owned by the Ohio Historical Society and located on a tract of fenced green space approximately one-acre in size. The mound, excavated by Clarence Loveberry in 1897, was originally about 25' (and now is 19.5') high and 95' in diameter. The mound is of historic significance because it is similar in size and shape to the now obliterated Adena Mound. (Adena Mound was located about 1 mile west of Story Mound on Adena, the estate of Thomas Worthington, a prominent politician of early Ohio. The Adena Mound was destroyed in 1901, but it produced artifacts considered so truly representative of the builders of the region's conical mounds that the name of the estate and mound came to be applied to the culture.)

Story Mound is also of historic significance because it provided archeologists with the first documentation of the circular house plan used by the Adena. The excavation of Story Mound uncovered post holes of a circular house 15' in diameter. This circular building form is now considered diagnostic of Adena domestic and ceremonial architecture.

DIRECTIONS: Exit U.S. Route 35 at Ohio 104 (Camp Sherman Memorial Highway). Go S on Camp Sherman Memorial Highway-High Street .8 mi to Allen Avenue, W on Allen Avenue .5 mi to Delano Avenue. S on Delano Avenue one block to Story Mound on E side of road. Curbside parking is available on Delano Avenue (Figure 66).

PUBLIC USE: Season and hours: The mound and interpretative sign can be viewed year round during daylight hours. **Restrictions:** The site is fenced and visitors are not permitted on the grounds.

FOR ADDITIONAL INFORMATION: Contact: Ohio Historical Society, 1985 Velma Avenue, Columbus, OH 43211, 614-466-1500.

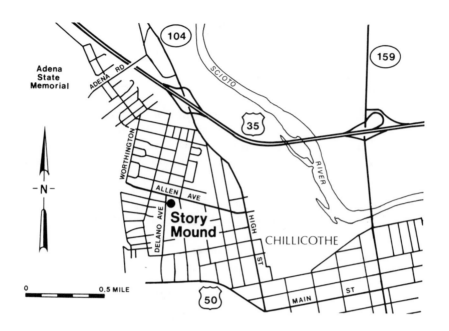

Figure 66. Location of Story Mound.

37. Tiltonsville Cemetery Mound

Adena burial mound
Tiltonsville, Jefferson County, Ohio

The Tiltonsville, or Hodgen's, Cemetery Mound is located on Arn Avenue, about 1,000' west of the Ohio River. This conical mound is 13' high and 80' in basal diameter. This mound is unusual in that it is located on the floodplain of the Ohio; normally Adena mounds are located on upland sites.

DIRECTIONS: Exit Ohio Route 7 at Tiltonsville-Farm Lane, go .15 mi E to Walden Street (old Ohio Route 7), then N on Walden .1 mi to Arn Avenue, then E on Arn Avenue 250'. The cemetery is on S side of Arn Avenue (Figure 67).

FOR ADDITIONAL INFORMATION: Contact: Village of Tiltonsville, Tiltonsville, OH 43963, 614-859-2730.

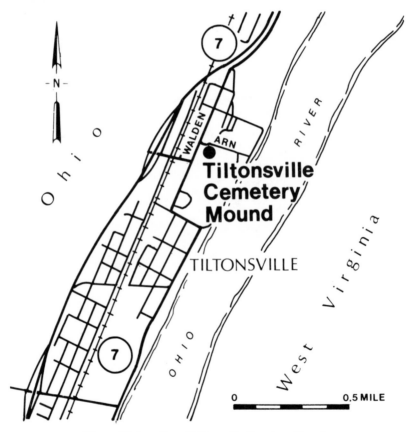

Figure 67. Location of Tiltonsville Cemetery Mound.

38. Tremper Mound

Hopewell burial mound
Scioto County, Ohio

This unique mound is located on a high terrace along the extreme western edge of the lower Scioto Valley, on what was once the estate of Senator William D. Tremper of Portsmouth. It originally was enclosed by a nearly square embankment measuring 420' × 440', with a single opening to the southeast. The mound was long thought to be an effigy mound, possibly an elephant or tapir, but William C. Mills's 1915 excavation revealed that the irregular shape was due to the structure of the underlying charnel house. Over 600 postmolds outlined a multichambered oval building 200' × 100' with several "wings" added to it (see Figure 12c). The maximum height of the mound was only 8.5', with its lowest parts at the eastern end and the projecting points being only about 1' high.

Many similarities exist between Tremper Mound and the Mound of the Pipes in the Mound City Group. In fact, Mills speculated that emigrants from Mound City may have constructed Tremper. In the middle chamber of the eastern "wings" was a cache of 136 pipes — all ritually broken. A smaller group of 9 unbroken pipes were discovered elsewhere. All but 4 were made of Ohio pipestone mined locally. About 90 were effigies of native animals, the rest being plain platform pipes. Some of the delicate bird effigy pipes had been broken by use and repaired with copper.

Unique to Tremper Mound was the use of communal depositories for the dead and their grave offerings rather than the individual burials characteristic of other Hopewell sites. Funerary use of Tremper was not limited by available floor space as was the case in other charnel houses, and Mills estimated that over 375 cremations were contained in the 4 communal graves. These constitute the greatest number of burials recorded in a single Hopewell burial mound.

The mound was completely restored after excavation, but the site is undeveloped and is privately owned. The mound is located on a low hill to the west of, and slightly above the level of, Ohio Routes 73 and 104, but it is in an open field, it is marked by a sign and it can be seen from the road immediately south of where Ohio Routes 73 and 104 converge.

DIRECTIONS: Combined Ohio Routes 73 and 104 pass the mound, separating 0.1 mile N of the site. This is a two lane highway. Caution should be exercised when viewing the mound, as traffic can be heavy at times. No formal parking is available (Figure 68).

PUBLIC USE: Restrictions: Private property. Do not enter without permission of the landowner.

FOR ADDITIONAL INFORMATION: Read: Mills, W. C. 1916. "Exploration of the Tremper Mound," Ohio Archaeological and Historical Quarterly, vol. 25, pp. 262-398.

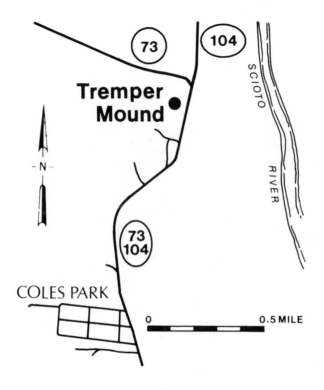

Figure 68. Location of Tremper Mound.

39. Williams Mound

(?)Adena burial mound
Homer, Licking County, Ohio

The Williams Mound, also known as the Dixon Mound, is a privately owned feature lying within the village of Homer in north-central Licking County. This single, conical mound is 15' high and has a basal diameter of 80'; it is located on an upland site not far from a bluff that descends to the floodplain of the North Fork of the Licking River. It is presently covered with low growing vegetation and a few small trees. The mound has not been excavated, so the cultural identity of its builders can not be confirmed. The size, shape and context of the mound, however, suggest that it is probably an Adena burial mound and, if so, it is one of only a few such features remaining in Licking County. This mound can be seen easily from municipal streets in Homer.

DIRECTIONS: Follow Ohio Route 661 14 mi N from Granville or 9 mi S from South Vernon (located 1 mi S of Mt. Vernon), to the center of Homer, then W on Licking County Route 19 (Homer Road N.W.) for .35 mi, then SE onto South Street (which intersects Route 19 at an oblique angle). The mound is on the S side of South Street behind the large yellow house (Figure 69).

PUBLIC USE: Restrictions: Private property. Obtain permission from the landowner before entering the property.

FOR ADDITIONAL INFORMATION: Contact: Ohio Historical Society, 1985 Velma Avenue, Columbus, OH 43211, 614-466-1500.

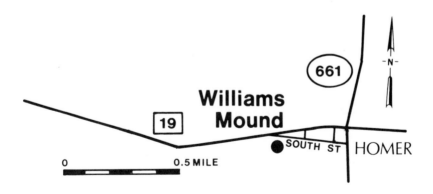

Figure 69. Location of Williams Mound.

111

40. Wright Brothers Memorial Mound Group

Adena (?)burial mounds
Greene County, Ohio

The six Adena mounds that constitute the Wright Brothers Memorial Mound Group are located near the western and northern edges of a hilltop immediately west of the Wright Brothers Memorial. These mounds vary from 1.7' high and 20' in basal diameter to 4.2' high and 50' in basal diameter. These mounds represent one of the finer clusters of Adena mounds that remain.

DIRECTIONS: Exit Ohio Route 444 onto Kauffman Road eastbound, go .15 mi E on Kauffman Road, then about 250' S on M Street to Gate 15B. Entrance to Wright Brothers Memorial is to the W of Gate 15B. The mounds are beyond the end of the Memorial drive (Figure 70).

FOR ADDITIONAL INFORMATION: Contact: Terry Lucas, Environmental Planning Office, 2750th Air Base Wing, Civil Engineering Squadron (DEEX), Wright Patterson Air Force Base, OH 45433, 513-257-7152.

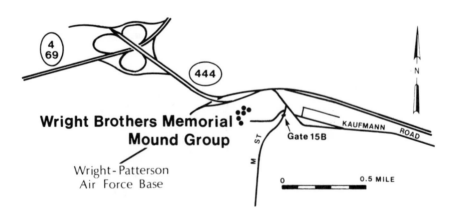

Figure 70. Location of Wright Brothers Memorial Mound Group.

41. Zaleski State Forest

Adena burial mound and earthworks
Vinton County, Ohio

Zaleski Mound I, also known as the Ranger Station Mound, is a conical feature that measures 14.4′ high and about 80′ in basal diameter. The mound is located in Zaleski State Forest, west of the Zaleski Elementary School near the forest manager's residence. The mound now has several large trees growing upon it. A driveway (State Forest Road 17) loops past the manager's residence and the mound, which is identified with a sign. Another mound — a small circle — can be seen along the Zaleski State Forest Backpack Trail. This feature is not accessible by motor vehicle, and it lies about 6 miles from the trailhead.

DIRECTIONS: From the intersection of Ohio Routes 278 and 677 in Zaleski, follow Route 278 N .3 mi, then go W at Zaleski Elementary School for .2 mi into Zaleski State Forest (via State Forest Road 17) and Mound I. Parking is available near the mound (Figure 71). The trailhead for the Zaleski backpack trail is located alongside Route 278 5 mi N of Zaleski. Parking is available at the trailhead.

FOR ADDITIONAL INFORMATION: Contact: Forest Manager, Zaleski State Forest, General Delivery, Zaleski, OH 45698, 614-596-5781.

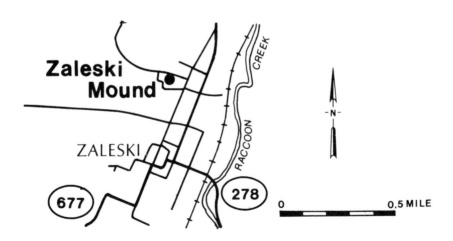

Figure 71. Location of Zaleski State Forest Mound.

SECTION III

SOURCES OF ADDITIONAL INFORMATION

MUSEUM EXHIBITS

The following museums (in addition to those at sites listed in Section II of this book) currently have exhibits that interpret the archeology of the Adena and Hopewell Indians. These exhibits are normally parts of larger exhibits dealing with the archeology of the eastern United States or more localized regions, and therefore present the mound building cultures in their chronological and geographical context. All of the museums except those marked with an asterisk (*) have a modest charge for admission. Most of the museums will provide group tours if such tours are requested well in advance of the tour date.

1. Cincinnati Museum of Natural History, 1720 Gilbert Avenue, Cincinnati, Ohio 45202, 513-621-3889. Hours: Tuesday through Saturday: 9:00 AM-5:00 PM; Sunday: 12:30-5:00 PM. Closed Mondays and national holidays.
2. Cleveland Museum of Natural History, Wade Oval, University Circle, Cleveland, Ohio 44106, 216-231-4600. Hours: Tuesday, Thursday through Saturday: 10:00 AM-5:00 PM; Wednesday: 10:00 AM-10:00 PM; Sunday: 1:00-5:30 PM. Closed major holidays.
3. Field Museum of Natural History, Roosevelt Road at Lake Shore Drive, Chicago, Illinois 60605, 312-922-9410. Hours: Daily, 9:00 AM-5:00 PM. Closed New Years Day, Thanksgiving, Christmas.
4. Glenn A. Black Laboratory of Archaeology*, 9th and Fess Streets, Indiana University, Bloomington, Indiana 47405, 812-335-9544. Hours: Monday through Friday: 8:00 AM-5:00 PM; Saturday-Sunday: 1:00-4:30 PM through the adjacent William Hammond Mathers Museum. Closed national holidays.
5. Museum of Anthropology*, Lafferty Hall, University of Kentucky, Lexington, Kentucky 40506, 606-257-7112. Hours: Monday through Friday: 8:00 AM-4:30 PM. Closed weekends and state holidays.
6. The Museum of Indian Heritage, 6040 De Long Road, Indianapolis, Indiana 46254, 317-293-4488. Hours: Tuesday through Sunday: 10:00 AM-5:00 PM. Closed Mondays, New Years Day, Easter, Thanksgiving and Christmas.
7. Museum of the American Indian-Heye Foundation, Broadway at 155th Street, New York, New York 10032, 212-283-2420. Hours: Tuesday through Saturday, 10:00 AM-5:00 PM; Sunday, 1:00-5:00 PM. Closed legal holidays.
8. Ohio Historical Center, Interstate 71 and 17th Avenue, Columbus, Ohio 43211, 614-466-1500. Hours: Monday through Saturday: 9:00 AM-5:00 PM; Sunday: 10:00 AM-5:00 PM. Closed Thanksgiving and Christmas.

(A new exhibit on the archeology of Ohio opened at the Ohio Historical Center on September 13, 1986. This exhibit represents the most detailed and comprehensive exhibit presently available to the public on Adena and Ohio Hopewell archeology. A special feature of the new exhibit is the presence of four computerized modules that allow visitors individually to test, and broaden, their knowledge of archeological and anthropological concepts and facts.)

PUBLICATIONS

The books and articles listed here are representative of professional and popular publications available on the Adena and Hopewell Indians. This list includes the most important publications of the 19th Century, at least one site report for the mounds listed in Section II of this book (if such reports are available and reasonably current), and other 20th Century publications that present recent or modern views on the archeology of the Adena or Hopewell. The actual list of titles dealing with these Indians is, of course, quite lengthy, but use of the publications listed here will introduce the reader or researcher to the literature on the Adena and Hopewell Indians.

Historical Perspectives

Atwater, Caleb. 1820. "Description of the antiquities discovered in the state of Ohio and other western states." Archaeologia Americana: Transactions and Collections of the American Antiquarian Society, vol. 1, pp. 109-251.

Mills, William C. 1914. Archaeological atlas of Ohio. Columbus: Ohio State Archaeological and Historical Society.

Schoolcraft, H. R. 1851. Historical and statistical information respecting the history, conditions, and prospects of the Indian tribes of the United States. Philadelphia: Lippincott, Grambo and Co. 6 vols.

Squier, Ephriam G., and Edwin H. Davis. 1848. Ancient monuments of the Mississippi Valley. Washington, D.C.: Smithsonian Contributions to Knowledge 1.

Shetrone, Henry C. 1930. The Mound-builders. New York: Appleton-Century.

Thomas, Cyrus. 1894. Report on the mound explorations of the Bureau of Ethnology. Washington, D.C.: Bureau of American Ethnology, Twelfth Annual Report, 1890-91.

Context and Overview

Fitting, James E. 1978. "Regional cultural development, 300 B.C. to A.D. 1000." Pp. 44-57 in William C. Sturtevant (ed.), Handbook of North American Indians; vol. 15 — Northeast. Washington, D.C.: Smithsonian Institution.

Jennings, Jesse D. 1968. Prehistoric man in North America. New York: McGraw-Hill.

Lilly, E. 1937. Prehistoric antiquities of Indiana. Indianapolis: Indiana Historical Society.

Murphy, James L. 1975. An archeological history of the Hocking Valley. Athens: Ohio University Press.

Potter, Martha A. 1968. Ohio's prehistoric peoples. Columbus: Ohio Historical Society.

Stuart, George E. 1972. "Mounds: riddles from the Indian past." National Geographic Magazine, vol. 142, pp. 782-801.

Silverberg, Robert. 1986. The mound builders. Athens: Ohio University Press.

Starr, S. F. 1960. "The archaeology of Hamilton County, Ohio." Journal of the Cincinnati Museum of Natural History, vol. 23, no. 1.

Tuck, James A. 1978. "Regional cultural development, 3000 to 300 B.C." Pp. 28-43 *in* William C. Sturtevant (ed.), Handbook of North American Indians; vol. 15 — Northeast. Washington, D.C.: Smithsonian Institution.

Current Views

Brose, David S., and l omi Greber. 1979. Hopewell archaeology: the Chillicothe conference. Kent, Ohio: Kent State University Press. (This volume contains a collection of 34 articles dealing with Adena and Hopewell archeology, and an extensive list of references.)

Carlson, John B. 1979. "Hopewell — prehistoric America's golden age." Early Man, Winter issue.

Dragoo, Don W. 1963. "Mounds for the Dead." Annals of Carnegie Museum, vol. 37.

Hively, Ray, and Robert Horn. 1982. "Geometry and astronomy in prehistoric Ohio." Archaeoastronomy, no. 4, pp. S1-S20.

Hively, Ray, and Robert Horn. 1984. "Hopewellian geometry and astronomy at High Bank." Archaeoastronomy, no. 7, pp. S85-S100.

Marshall, James A. 1979. "Geometry of the Hopewell earthworks." Early Man. Spring issue, pp. 1-8.

Prufer, Olaf H. 1964. "The Hopewell cult." Scientific American, vol. 211. no. 6, pp. 90-102.

Site Reports

Baby, Raymond S., and Suzanne M. Langlois. 1979. "Seip Mound State Memorial: nonmortuary aspects of Hopewell." Pp. 16-18 *in* D. S. Brose and N. Greber (eds.), Hopewell archaeology. Kent, Ohio: Kent State University Press.

Greber, N'omi. 1979. "A comparative study of site morphology and burial patterns at Edwin Harness Mound and Seip mounds 1 and 2." Pp. 27-38 *in* D. S. Brose and N. Greber (eds.), Hopewell archaeology. Kent, Ohio: Kent State University Press.

Greenman, E. F. 1932. "Excavation of the Coon Mound and an analysis of the Adena culture." Ohio State Archaeological and Historical Quarterly, vol. 41, pp. 366-523.

Hemmings, E. Thomas. 1984. "Fairchance Mound and village: An early middle Woodland settlement in the Upper Ohio Valley." West Virginia Archeologist, vol. 36, no. 1, pp. 3-68 (including two appendices).

Hemmings, E. Thomas. 1984. "Investigations at Grave Creek Mound 1975-76: a sequence for mound and moat construction." West Virginia Archeologist, vol. 36, no. 2, pp. 3-49.

Kellar, James H. 1969. "New excavations at Mounds State Park — life in Indiana 2,000 years ago." Outdoor Indiana, vol. 34, no. 7, pp. 4-9.

Mills, William C. 1902. "Excavation of the Adena Mound." Ohio Archaeological and Historical Quarterly, vol. 10, pp. 451-479.

Mills, William C. 1909. "Explorations of the Seip Mound." Ohio Archaeological and Historical Quarterly, vol. 18, pp. 269-321.

Mills, William C. 1916. "Exploration of the Tremper Mound." Ohio Archaeological and Historical Quarterly, vol. 25, pp. 262-398.

Mills, William C. 1922. "Exploration of the Mound City Group." Ohio Archaeological and Historical Quarterly, vol. 31, pp. 423-584.

Moorehead, Warren K. 1922. "The Hopewell Mound Group of Ohio." Field Museum of Natural History, Anthropological Series, vol. 6, pp. 73-184.

Morgan, Richard G. 1970. Fort Ancient. Columbus: Ohio Historical Society.

Morgan, Richard G., and Edward S. Thomas. 1948. Fort Hill. Columbus: Ohio State Archaeological and Historical Society.

Norona, Delf. 1962. Moundsville's Mammoth Mound. Special publication of the West Virginia Archeological Society, no. 6.

Shetrone, Henry C. 1926. "Exploration of the Hopewell group of prehistoric earthworks." Ohio Archaeological and Historical Quarterly, vol. 35, pp. 1-227.

Shetrone, Henry C., and Emerson F. Greenman. 1931. "Explorations of the Seip group of prehistoric earthworks." Ohio Archaeological and Historical Quarterly, vol. 40, pp. 343-509.

Swartz, B. K., Jr. 1976. "Mounds State Park." Central States Archaeological Journal, vol. 23, pp. 26-32.

Vickery, Kent D. 1970. "Preliminary report on the excavation of the 'Great Mound' at Mounds State Park in Madison County, Indiana." Proceedings of the Indiana Academy of Science for 1969, vol. 79, pp. 75-82.

Webb, William S. 1941. "Mt. Horeb earthworks, site 1 and the Drake Mound, site 11, Fayette County, Kentucky." University of Kentucky Papers in Anthropology and Archaeology, vol. 5, no. 2.

Other Relevant Publications

DeLong, Richard M. 1972. Bedrock geology of the Flint Ridge area, Licking and Muskingum counties, Ohio. Ohio Division of Geological Survey Report of Investigations no. 84. Color map, 1″ = 2,000′; one sheet with text.

Hooge, Paul, and others. n.d. Discovering the prehistoric mound builders of Licking County, Ohio. Newark: The Licking County Archaeological and Landmarks Society. One sheet, color, text with maps and other illustrations.

Reidel, Stephen P. 1975. Bedrock geology of the Serpent Mound cryptoexplosion structure, Adams, Highland, and Pike counties, Ohio. Ohio Division of Geological Survey Report of Investigations no. 95. Color map, 1″ = 1,000′; one sheet with text.

Stout, Wilbur, and R. A. Schoenlaub. 1945. The occurrence of flint in Ohio. Ohio Division of Geological Survey, fourth series — Bulletin 46.

TOPOGRAPHIC MAPS

Topographic maps show mound sites in their modern physical and cultural context. Listed below are the names of the topographic maps (technically called quadrangles) upon which are located each of the sites described in Section II of this book. All or some of the mounds at the sites marked with an asterisk (*) are labeled on the respective maps; the locations of mounds at the other sites usually can be determined by reference to the location descriptions given in Section II. All maps named here are in the U. S. Geological Survey's 7.5 minute (7.5', or 1:24,000 scale) series.

1. Adena Park — Centerville, Kentucky
2. Ashland Central Park — Ashland, Kentucky-Ohio
3. Camden Park Mound — Catlettsburg, Kentucky-Ohio-West Virginia
4. Campbell Mound* — Southwest Columbus, Ohio
5. Elk Lick Road Mound — Batavia, Ohio
6. Enon Mound* — Donnelsville, Ohio
7. Fairmount Mound — Thornville, Ohio
8. Flint Ridge State Memorial — Glenford, Ohio
9. Fort Ancient State Memorial* — Oregonia, Ohio
10. Fort Hill State Memorial — Sinking Creek, Ohio
11. Glenford Fort — Glenford, Ohio and Somerset, Ohio
12. Grave Creek Mound* — Moundsville, Ohio-West Virginia
13. Hartman Mound* — The Plains, Ohio
14. Highbanks Park Earthworks — Powell, Ohio
15. Hueston Woods Campground Mound — College Corner, Indiana-Ohio
16. Indian Mound Campground — The Plains, Ohio
17. Indian Mound Park — Cedarville, Ohio
18. Indian Mounds Park — Southeast.Columbus, Ohio
19. Marietta Earthworks* — Marietta, Ohio-West Virginia
20. Miamisburg Mound State Memorial* — Miamisburg, Ohio
21. Mound Cemetery Mound — Chester, Ohio-West Virginia
22. Mound City Group National Monument* — Andersonville, Ohio (Small parts of the monument also are mapped on the Chillicothe West and Kingston, Ohio, quadrangles.)
23. Mounds State Park* — Middletown, Indiana (Small parts of the park also are mapped on the Anderson South, Indiana, quadrangle.)
24. Newark Earthworks* — Newark, Ohio
25. Norwood Mound — Cincinnati East, Ohio
26. Orator's Mound — Yellow Springs, Ohio
27. Piketon Mound Cemetery — Piketon, Ohio
28. Portsmouth Mound Park — Portsmouth, Kentucky-Ohio
29. Reynolds Mound — Raven Rock, Ohio-West Virginia
30. Seip Mound State Memorial* — Morgantown, Ohio
31. Serpent Mound State Memorial* — Sinking Creek, Ohio
32. Shawnee Lookout Park — Lawrenceburg, Indiana-Kentucky-Ohio
33. Shawnee Reservation Mound* — Saint Albans, West Virginia
34. Shorts Woods Park Mound — Burlington, Kentucky-Ohio

35. South Charleston Mound* — Charleston West, West Virginia
36. Story Mound — Chillicothe East, Ohio
37. Tiltonsville Cemetery Mound — Tiltonsville, Ohio-West Virginia
38. Tremper Mound* — West Portsmouth, Ohio
39. Williams Mound — Homer, Ohio
40. Wright Brothers Memorial Mound Group — Fairborn, Ohio
41. Zaleski Mound Group* — Zaleski, Ohio

Topographic maps may be purchased from the following government offices. Order by specifying name(s) of quadrangle, state, and scale or series desired. All mail orders must be prepaid, including sales tax, postage, and handling charges as necessary. Some maps are also available from various local private and government distributors.

1. U. S. Geological Survey, Map Distribution, Federal Center, Building 41, Box 25286, Denver, Colorado 80225, 303-236-7477.

Any of the maps listed above may be ordered from this source. Maps cost $2.50 each. There is a $1.00 handling charge if the total order is less than $10.00. Checks should be made payable to U. S. Geological Survey.

2. Publications Section, Indiana Geological Survey, 611 North Walnut Grove, Bloomington, Indiana 47405, 812-335-7636.

Only Indiana maps can be obtained from this source. Maps cost $2.50 each. Postage and handling charges are additional.

3. Kentucky Geological Survey, University of Kentucky, 311 Breckinridge Hall, Lexington, Kentucky 40506-0056, 606-257-3196.

Only Kentucky maps can be obtained from this source. Maps cost $3.60 each. Sales tax and shipping charges are additional.

4. Ohio Division of Natural Resources, Division of Geological Survey, Fountain Square, Building B, Columbus, Ohio 43225, 614-265-6605.

Only Ohio maps can be obtained from this source. Maps cost $2.50 each. Sales tax and handling charges are additional.

5. West Virginia Geological and Economic Survey, P. O. Box 879, Morgantown, West Virginia 26507-0879, 304-594-2331.

Only West Virginia maps can be obtained from this source. Maps cost $2.50 each. Sales tax and shipping charges are additional.

INDEX

128

Tarleton, Ohio 33
Tarleton Cross Mound 33
The Plains, Ohio 57, 58, 59
Thomas, Cyrus 29, 30, 52, 104
Tiltonsville, Ohio 7, 26, 108
Tiltonsville Cemetery Mound 34, 108
Toltecs 28
Tremper, William D. 109
Tremper Mound 19, 20, 21, 34, 109, 110

University of Kentucky 35, 36

Vikings 28
Vinton County, Ohio 113

Wabash River 21
Warren County, Ohio 47
Washington County, Ohio 67
Wayne County, West Virginia 38
Webb, William S. 29, 35
Wheeling, West Virginia 7, 11, 34
White River 7, 11, 77, 78
Whitewater River 7, 77
Whittlesey, Charles 28, 68, 80
Williams Mound 26, 34, 111
Williamson Mound 64, 65
Wolfe's Plains, Ohio 7, 10, 15, 57, 58
Wolfe's Plains Earthworks 34, 56, 57, 59
Woodland Culture 5, 60
Woodland Period 6
Woodruff Connett Mounds 57
Works Progress Administration 35
Worthington, Thomas 5, 12, 106
Wright Brothers Memorial 112
Wright Brothers Memorial Mound Group 34, 112
Wright Earthworks 82
Wright Earthworks State Memorial 82, 83

Yellow Springs, Ohio 85

Zaleski Mound I 34, 113
Zaleski State Forest 34, 113